Sounds of Singing
Teacher's Book
Y5-6/P6-7

Alison Ley

Published in 2004 by:
Nelson Thornes Ltd
Delta Place
27 Bath Road
CHELTENHAM
GL53 7TH
United Kingdom

04 05 06 07 08 / 10 9 8 7 6 5 4 3 2 1

A catalogue record for this book is available from the British Library

ISBN 0–17–427100–X

Music notation by Linda Lancaster Music Setting, Huddersfield
Page make-up by Florence Production Limited, Stoodleigh, Devon

Printed in Croatia by Zrinski

Contents

Foreword

These are interesting times for singing, and particularly for singing in school. Challenged by exciting advances in instrumental music and latterly in music technology, and sidelined by popular musical culture, 'choral' singing has over the last half-century lost its natural place at the centre of children's musical experience.

Boys in particular are reluctant to sing, for complex sociological and cultural reasons. At the same time our innate tribal need to communicate through song is there as much as ever, as evidenced from the football field to the opera house.

The good news is that we have a change in the tide. It was a joy for me to be a member of the working group which created the first National Curriculum for music back in 1991, and which provided the chance to state clearly the place of singing at the core of musical activity and of learning. There is right now a unique opportunity to develop new ways to exploit our most economical natural musical resource, the singing voice.

The biggest single issue now is helping teachers to deliver. There is an urgent need to help build their confidence and skills, by providing user-friendly source materials and schemes of work. Here we have a splendid answer.

Sounds of Singing works in the best sense from the ground upwards.

The secret is lateral thinking – new strategies to subvert the reluctance of pupils to come out of hiding and express themselves vocally, and to develop their singing skills step by step, alongside their enjoyment in working through appealingly presented material.

Each lesson introduces an aspect of singing technique, a new musical style, the opportunity to improvise and create sounds and to develop musicianship and memory. Listening and performing go side by side here, and the activities and their outcomes are presented in a way which even the most inexperienced teacher will find supportive and non-threatening.

The use of CD performances of pieces is a masterstroke, and the performances are of a high quality too. Backing tracks are separated from the vocals, offering a variety of learning methods.

All in all, *Sounds of Singing* is a magnificent concept, and an invaluable resource for all primary music teachers. With materials like this, we can take the tide at the flood, and get surfing.

Mike Brewer OBE
Musical Director, National Youth Choirs
of Great Britain and Laudibus

All about Sounds of Singing

The task ahead

The voice is the one musical instrument that we all possess. It is portable, requires little maintenance and is a great means of expression. In an ideal world, teachers would sing happily and uninhibitedly with their children (and some do), but many of us do not find this very easy. The whole process involves both teacher and pupil in physical skills, memory skills, listening skills, language skills and vocal skills. Learning songs to practise all these skills can only be pleasurable if the materials used are reassuringly accessible and stimulating, are carefully graded, come in bite-size portions and give clear guidance on how to get the very best out of every song. Above all the whole process must be made enjoyable. *Sounds of Singing* provides all this.

Who can use Sounds of Singing?

Sounds of Singing is for both the musically experienced and musically inexperienced primary classroom teacher and is derived from the author's years of experience both with teaching singing and in helping others to do so.

Sounds of Singing and Sounds of Music

Sounds of Singing has been carefully designed to be a free-standing course, for use on its own or in conjunction with a school's own music programme or other published resources. However, users of *Sounds of Music* – a classroom music scheme for primary schools – will see how easily the two resources dovetail together, resulting in a truly comprehensive solution for primary music education. More information about the relationship with *Sounds of Music* appears on page 91.

Universal links

Singing is universal. While there may be differences of expression in the curriculum requirements and guidelines of different countries, in essence they are much the same and it is this common purpose that forms the basis of *Sounds of Singing*. Charts showing the correlation between the course and current curriculum documents are available free of charge. Please see page 89 for details.

The structure

There are three levels of *Sounds of Singing*: R–Y2/P1–3, Y3–4/P4–5, and Y5–6/P6–7. At each level there is a comprehensive teacher's book and a set of audio CDs.

The teacher's book is divided into chapters, concentrating on different aspects of singing, and each chapter is itself divided into lessons. An introductory page at the beginning of each chapter sets out the scope and focus of the lessons. The term 'lesson' is used loosely: you may indeed choose to teach all the suggested activities in one session, but equally you may prefer to tackle them in discrete chunks, perhaps in odd moments during the week or as part of a music lesson covering a broader range of topics.

Questions and answers

Within the lessons, questions have been devised for you to ask the children. The answers to these questions are in italicised brackets. The body of the text not only provides easily understood lesson notes but it also includes clarification and explanation of the more musically specialised matters.

Sequence, progression and differentiation

It is suggested that you teach the activities within a lesson in the order they are presented here, but it is not necessary to teach the lessons themselves in the printed sequence. All the lessons in *Sounds of Singing* are appropriate for the stated age range and there is careful progression from one book to the next. Within each lesson there is a wide range of activities that will suit all levels of ability, but much of the differentiation will naturally be by outcome.

Learning by rote

All activities for R–Y2/P1–3 are taught by rote. In Y3–4/P4–5 there are some references and learning experiences related to notation, and more again for Y5–6/P6–7. However, the most important and essential elementary skill is listening, because children cannot develop their singing without the ability to hear themselves, the group they are singing with, and their role models (teacher or recordings). You can, of course, use the given notation in any way you wish – however, the focus of this book is on aural skills.

Learning the words

Learning lyrics by rote is not a musical activity. This book aims to show you how to teach a song so that learning words for homework becomes obsolete. If you follow the lesson plans, the songs are taught in bite-size portions enabling the children to memorise one short section easily before going on to the next short section. The other learning method that is sometimes used is to play the song as background music and let it slowly filter into the mind as if by osmosis.

Achievement

At the end of each lesson, 'achievement' points are identified to help you recognise what can be assessed and how effectively a child is developing his or her musical skills and understanding. Do not go into overload: at any one time, assess just a few children's achievements and focus on just one or two points.

What's on the page

The consistent, 'at a glance' layout of the lessons makes *Sounds of Singing* exceptionally easy to use.

ideas to help children warm up their voices and practise vocal techniques

hints and tips to support non-specialist teachers

clear objectives to focus teaching and planning

list of resources and background information to save preparation time

points to check for assessment and planning

CHAPTER 4

Frameworks

Lesson 2

Geordie's Penker and Jikel 'Emaweni

Focus

Listening with care to different speech sounds. Singing in a regional accent. Writing words phonetically. Identifying and making click sounds. Singing in a foreign language.

Resources

CD 2 tracks 14, 15, 16, 17; song sheets 27, 28, 29.

About the song

Geordie's Penker.

This humorous folk song is sung in a regional accent and uses dialect words. A 'penker' is a marble, 'double row' is a double terrace of houses, and a 'cundy' is a drainpipe (conduit).

Jikel 'Emaweni

This is a work song from South Africa. It would be sung to accompany the rhythmic movements of a group employed in building, digging, quarrying and so on.

Activities

Copying a regional accent

Play Geordie's Penker (track 14) and ask the children to listen very carefully to the pronunciation of the words, in particular the last line of each verse. Now ask them to say the last line, copying the accent exactly. Play the song again and let them join in, singing the last line and still mimicking the accent.

Aids to pronunciation

Many folk and traditional songs are passed down from generation to generation through the aural tradition. Sometimes the exact pronunciation of the words is written down phonetically.

Arrange the children into small groups and appoint a scribe to each group. Play Nonsense Words (track 15) and ask them to listen very carefully to the pronunciation of each word. Pause after each word so that each group can discuss how they will write it phonetically. Discuss various phonetic versions of the same word, including the following examples: dopolop, teckizing, klacack, mowa, yickoo, splishow, flarelala, brrrk. Decide which spelling works the best and why. Do not worry about the phonetic realisation conforming to 'standard' phonetics; as long as the children can understand their own representation, that is all that is required. Now listen again to Geordie's Penker and ask them to write down the last line in phonetics.

Singing in a foreign language

It is often easier for a group to sing in a foreign language than in their own, as everyone can learn to pronounce the words in exactly the same way with no individual accents to eliminate. Play Jikel 'Emaweni (track 16) several times to familiarise the children with the melody and ask them to identify exactly where the clicks come in the words of the song (see song sheet 28). Play track 17, pausing after each line to allow the children to copy exactly and to memorise the words they hear on the recording. Once the children know the words write the phonetic lyrics on the board (written under the lyrics) so that they can relate the written word to the aural sound.

Achievement

Can listen accurately to different speech sounds. Can copy a regional accent. Can write vocal sounds phonetically. Can identify click sounds. Can sing foreign words with accuracy.

opportunities for children to apply their skills and musicianship to their singing

In addition to the lesson plans, the book contains:

- song sheets which may be photocopied or projected for whole-class or group use
- advice on planning a singing session
- general advice on teaching singing
- a collection of generic warm-up activities which are not specific to any one particular song, but which can be used at any time
- general advice on the value of music, movement and dance
- a glossary of technical terms
- information about links with current curriculum guidelines and requirements, and with *Sounds of Music*
- an analysis of the songs and listening extracts.

The recordings

Recordings on audio CDs support each lesson. To get the best out of these recordings it is important to have a good CD player, preferably with a balance control. The quality of the sound makes a big difference to a child's response to any music. These recordings provide all the music mentioned in the lessons, including:

- **Warm-up exercises and games**
  These exercises prepare the voice for singing and teach specific vocal techniques. You might use these recordings to help you learn the warm-ups yourself, so that you can sing them with the children, or you might prefer to play the recordings directly to the class.

- **Listening extracts**
  Extracts of a wide variety of singing (and other music) for listening activities to focus children's attention on specific vocal issues. These extracts are of an appropriate length for the age group and for the activity and save you the time and money required to build and select from a large listening library.

- **Songs**
  Songs that are performed to a high professional standard and that provide an excellent vocal model.

- **Instrumental accompaniments**
  The instrumental accompaniments are varied, stylistically apt and musically satisfying. If your CD has a balance control you can isolate either the singing or the accompaniment, which are recorded on the separate stereo tracks. This enables the class to perform a familiar song with the professional backing track but without the support of the recorded vocals. Conversely, you may wish to focus on the vocal line when children are learning a song. Listening to the backing tracks on their own also gives a greater insight into the interpretation of the song, and many backing tracks can also be used as music for creative dance.

Please note that it is illegal to make copies of the CDs under any circumstances. Additional CDs are available for separate purchase.

All about planning a singing session

The following tips may help you to plan a well-structured singing session:

Space

Make sure that you have enough space for the children to stand comfortably.

To sit or to stand?

It is best to stand, but when the children do sit, please try to use chairs. It is really difficult to sing sitting cross-legged on the floor: it is like being asked to run a marathon with your legs inside a sack!

Ventilation

A room that is too hot, too stuffy or too cold will have a detrimental effect on any singing.

Know your material

Before you teach any song, you must know the piece intimately. It is said that amateurs practise until they get it right, but professionals practise until they can't get it wrong. You may not be a professional singer, but you are a professional teacher or choral leader and you need to know your song back to front so that you can teach it with confidence and detect exactly what the children are singing – both the good bits and the not-so-good bits. The lesson plans make this easy for you and will tell you how to approach the song as well as making you aware of any likely problems.

Admire your reflection

Using a long mirror to watch yourself singing and conducting is mentioned in 'All about singing', but it is worth reinforcing that it is one of the most helpful methods of becoming familiar with your material. Better still, ask a friend to take a video of you.

Make teaching simple

In truth, it is not possible to direct, listen, control and support a group satisfactorily at the same time as playing the piano. The piano acts as a sound barrier between you and the children, and your concentration is divided between the keyboard and the children. Teach a song from the recording, or use a guitar, or sing the melody unaccompanied for the children to copy.

Demonstrate, don't verbalise

Try to demonstrate rather than going into lengthy verbal explanations. Once the children have a reasonable grasp of the melody, stop singing with them and listen for any mistakes before they become too well established. Constantly remind the children to listen to themselves so that they blend in with everybody else.

Separate the tracks

If you have a balance control on your CD player, listen to both the backing track and the vocals on their own. The vocals provide a good role model and a standard of excellence for the children to copy. The accompaniments help to establish the mood, style and character of a song and help them with their expression and interpretation. Use the backing tracks to support the singing, not to drown it out.

General warm-ups

Before embarking on any strenuous physical exercise, it is essential to loosen up and to 'warm up' in order to prevent injuries. It is equally important to start each singing session with one or two general loosening and warm-up activities. Examples can be found on page xviii.

Specific warm-ups

The warm-ups that precede each individual song are devised in order to help address the more challenging aspects of that specific song. Many of these warm-ups can be transferred and used at the beginning of other singing sessions. For instance, articulation and pitch skills learnt in one song could be adapted and transferred to improve the execution of another song.

First things first

Ensure that the main teaching points are contained in the early part of the session while the singers are fresh. Use familiar material later on in the session to refocus and motivate.

Grouping

Sometimes it is advisable to select groups randomly: for example, by the colour of their hair, by birthdays, by the initial letter of their name, by their favourite food and so on. At other times you may want to distribute your stronger singers among the different groups.

Recording

Recording the class on tape or mini disk allows for evaluation and useful discussion afterwards.

Memorising

It is always best to perform any song from memory. This not only affects the sound quality (good posture is maintained) but it also means that you have constant eye contact with the children. When the children are looking forward, it establishes a rapport with the audience, engaging them with much greater effect.

Setting the scene

When practising, it helps to sing to an imaginary audience, perhaps to a romantic couple dining out, or to the family at home, or in a cathedral, or in the park. You will need to adapt your performance to each imagined (or real) situation.

High standards

Establish high standards – children like to be part of something that is successful.

Less is more

It is better for the children to sing one song really well than to sing four or five songs in a mediocre manner.

A satisfying end

End the session on a high. Make sure that the singers go away with a sense of achievement.

Extra-curricular choirs

Extra-curricular choirs need not run every week of the school year – this is a big commitment for both you and the children and they can become disenchanted with the routine. Form a choir for special events and rehearse for about six to eight weeks before the event.

All about singing

You can, of course, skip these introductory pages, and still succeed in teaching the contents of this book, but please do take some time to read them as it is here that you will find basic singing skills clearly defined, and written in plain English. The information will help you to understand how you can improve your singing and, as a consequence, it will increase your confidence – whether you are singing in the classroom, on a concert platform, in the crowd at a football match or simply in the bath.

The process of singing

The process of singing is quite straightforward to understand:

* Lungs supply the air.
* Air causes vocal cords to vibrate which creates sound.
* Sound is amplified by resonating cavities i.e. nose, mouth, neck and chest.
* The tongue, lips and teeth articulate the sound.

Posture

Stand in an alert and balanced position with a long spine and knees very slightly flexed – i.e. not rigidly locked. Your head should be level and aligned with the spinal column. Your chest should be raised and your shoulders down and relaxed with your hands by your side. Aim for balance and freedom, not rigid and soldier-like with chest puffed out.

When sitting on a chair, sit forward, feet flat on the ground, adopt a good posture to keep the chest and lungs upright in order to maximise the lung capacity. If you sit back in a chair, your body will take on the shape of the chair, which makes unrestricted breathing difficult.

A smiley face

Sing with a smiling face – not a great big grin but more as if you are breathing in the scent of a sweet smelling rose: you are surprised at the delicious aroma. This expression lifts the whole of your face and not only does it look good, but it also feels good and helps to keep the singing in tune and create a pleasant tone.

All about breathing

There are three parts to successful breathing whilst singing:

1. breathing in
2. breathing out
3. breath management.

Three sets of muscles manage the flow of air:

1. the diaphragm, i.e. the muscle that separates your lungs from your stomach and which supports the lungs like an elastic platform.
2. the intercostal (rib) muscles above the diaphragm.
3. the abdominal muscles below the diaphragm, i.e. between the diaphragm and pelvis.

Together these muscles manage the flow of air provided to the vocal cords (in the larynx). This air causes the vocal cords to vibrate and a sound is produced. In a child, the vocal cords are like two fine and delicate flexible threads; in adults they are more like two pieces of a rubber band.

Breathing in

When we go about our normal daily business, we breathe without thinking about it. We take in a small amount of air and only use the top part of our lungs. When singing, we need to sing long notes and phrases, so we must have a plentiful supply of air. To acquire this, we will need to breathe deeply and utilise our full lung capacity.

When we breathe deeply, the abdominal muscles expand, the intercostal muscles open up the chest (including the sides and the back) and air floods in saturating the whole of our lungs from the bottom to the top. Think of it as filling a bottle with water. The shoulders should stay relaxed and still. We do not breathe with our shoulders.

To actually see how your physiology changes, stand in front of a mirror. Put one hand on your abdomen, below your navel, and the other hand on your side around your waist. Breathe in deeply through your mouth and nose. Can you see your abdomen, sides and chest expand and your shoulders stay still? Another way to feel this is to lie on your back on the floor and to put a small book on your stomach. Breathe in deeply and watch the book move. Yet another way to locate your abdominal muscles is by bending right over in your chair and breathing deeply in and out. You will feel the muscles expanding and contracting.

Breathing out and breath management

We have already seen that when we breathe in without thinking about it, we take small amounts of air into the top of our lungs. So, when we breathe out without thinking about it, the lungs and ribs 'collapse' and the small amount of air flows out.

We have also already established that when we sing, we need a lot of air in the lungs, however, we do need to ration the amount of air we expel, commensurate with exactly how much we need to use at any given time. To do this, we use our abdominal muscles to push air out of our lungs and to regulate the flow. Think of the lower abdominal muscles being the engine, and the air the petrol; the one controls the rate at which the other is used. Try putting your hand just ten centimetres in front of your mouth. Take a deep breath and blow on to your hand as if you were blowing up a balloon. Keep blowing a steady, even pressured stream of air until all the air has been used up. Keep your chest lifted and buoyant so that your ribs remain expanded, ready for the next intake of breath. Can you feel your abdominal muscles pushing the air out from the bottom of your lungs? Coughing quite vigorously may help you to locate those muscles and the associated physical sensation.

This controlled pressure from below the lungs is known as 'supporting the breath'. Good breath control is the secret to making a good sound.

You will notice that small children often sing with a very breathy tone, breathing in frequently and totally at random. This is because they do not know how to control the amount of air they expel at any one time. Try singing any song that you know with a breathy sound and hardly any melodic vocal sound. Now sing the same song without the breathy sound but with as much vocal sound as possible. In order to sing with very little superfluous breath escaping, you will have exercised some control over the rate of air flow. To do this you will have used the same mechanism described above. With regular practice, breath management can be improved until the sound becomes true and clear and long phrases can be sung.

Helping children to improve their breathing and breath control

Key Stage 1

Delving into the physiology of breathing would not be appropriate. You simply need to encourage the children to adopt a good singing position, to breathe low down (use the water bottle analogy), and to make sure that they have enough breath (and not too much) to last for the length of the phrase they are about to sing. Try not to say 'Take a big breath', as they are likely to pull in their abdomen, their shoulders will rise, they will create tension in their neck and throat, and they will probably only use the top half of their lungs. In this stance, they will have little control over the use of their air supply, and they will not make a very good sound. In other words they will take in breath, in exactly the opposite way to the low breathing technique described above. The best way is to ask them to take a drink of air or to take a deep breath or to breathe into their tummies.

Years 3 and 4

The children should begin to have more understanding of how to manage their breathing. Many children will know how to breathe deeply, and some children will be able to use their 'tummy' muscles to support the airflow for specific notes (e.g. high notes) or phrases (e.g. long phrases) or dynamics (e.g. passages that get louder).

Years 5 and 6

All children should clearly understand the principles of good breathing, and should be able to recognise the advantages of good breath management. Many children will be able to exercise good breath control, but do not expect them to automatically do this all the time. Professional singers spend years perfecting their breathing technique. Aim for silent, deep breathing and unanimity of breathing within a choir. Encourage the use of the abdominal muscles for specific notes and phrases (e.g. as above and in quiet passages, when singing large ascending melodic jumps, for accented notes and for downward scale passages).

Head and chest voice

We do not sing with our chest or our head! Every instrument has to have a resonating chamber to amplify the sound and the voice is no exception. The two main resonating areas are the chest and the head.

It is not possible to sing high notes using the chest voice; a sudden unattractive drop in volume occurs when higher notes are reached. Try asking a group of children to sing fairly loudly up a scale and notice the difference between the quality of the sound of the lower notes to that of the higher notes.

The light head voice is the voice that children will naturally use and the one that can be used across the whole range and for all styles of music. Children's natural chest voice does not have a lot of power and is quite quiet; this is why they force the sound when singing lower notes in order to achieve a greater volume. They use a kind of 'shouting' voice.

There is a place in some pop or rock songs, for using this stronger 'shouting' or 'belt' type of voice, but for classes and choirs, it is generally not advisable. It puts a strain on the vocal cords, is tiring to sustain, has a limited range and is not very musical. The children singing on the recordings of *Sounds of Singing* only once use their stronger chest voice and that is in Years 3 and 4, in the song, 'At the Hop' for the words 'Oh baby'. Volume will develop with age and experience rather than with forcing the vocal cords to belt out a song. To help projection, remember to pay close attention to posture and to breathing and ask the children to sing out – i.e. to sing to the other end of the room, not to shout to the other end of the room.

Singing in tune

Flat singing (singing under the note) often occurs when there is insufficient breath and insufficient support for the breath. It can also occur when singers are tired, when the room is hot and stuffy, when notes are pitched too high, on repeated notes, on descending phrases or simply when children have not had sufficient time to listen to the exact pitches they are being asked to sing. Remedy the problem by doing some physical exercises to re-energise the class. Pay attention to posture and breathing, ask the children to stand whilst singing, and to sing fairly quietly so that they can hear themselves. Play the 'flat' phrase several times on a pitched instrument or ask the children to listen to the recording so that they can hear and re-learn the correct pitches.

Sharp singing (singing higher than the note) is less common than flat singing and often occurs when children are anxious, when they are trying too hard, when they are singing high notes or when they are not listening carefully enough. To remedy the problem, do some relaxing exercises before having another go and play the 'sharp' phrase several times on a pitched instrument or listen to the recording so that the exact pitches can be heard and re-learned.

Articulation

To articulate with clarity, your face will need to be very flexible and your lips, tongue and teeth should work overtime, especially when singing in a large group. Try singing through a stiff 'letter box' mouth – notice how difficult it is to sing and to form the words. Silently mouth a sentence to an imaginary person at the other side of the room, and note the facial movement and physical sensation that precise and energetic enunciation requires. This is what is required when we sing.

Unified vowels

Tone is produced and carried on vowels, and vowel sounds are controlled by mouth shape. Sing the following vowels (on one long note) and notice how the position of your tongue, and your mouth shape (especially inside your mouth), changes with each vowel.

i as in need
e as in Ted
a as in part
o as in boat
u as in toot

Ideally every one should pronounce their vowels in the same way to produce the best tone quality and the best blend within a group of singers. Listen carefully for vowels that are obviously not unanimous and decide on the best pronunciation for your group of children and for the style of the song.

Expression

Good dynamics and expression 'make' a song. When deciding on the expressive qualities that you want to include, look at the words, feel the mood and find the main climax of the whole song. You can never sing too quietly, but you can sing too loudly.

Phrasing

Ensure that the children take the right amount of breath for each phrase (and not too much) so that it can be sung expressively and not peter out through lack of breath. Don't be afraid to shorten the length of a note at the end of a phrase to allow sufficient time to breathe before the next phrase begins.

Listening and vocal co-ordination

Singing is a physical activity and is really only an extension of speaking since it uses the same apparatus. Most children will hear pitches correctly but some children's vocal apparatus will not replicate that pitch. This is usually because, at some stage in that child's development, he or she has not had the opportunity to sing and to practise that basic skill. Just as some people are more skilled than others are at skipping or catching a ball, so it is that some can control their vocal apparatus better than others can. You can help children to improve their listening and singing co-ordination by asking them to copy your voice as you sing long continuous sounds at a pitch that is comfortably within their natural singing range. This could be quite a low pitch. Gradually extend the range and the number of notes. Do not exclude them from singing; they cannot improve if they do not practise and they will also feel very isolated.

Conducting

When you conduct a song, you direct the performers by using a variety of non-verbal gestures. Apart from using your hands and arms, other gestures will include eye contact, mouthing the words, nodding your head, using facial expressions and using your whole body to indicate mood.

Try to find time to work out what conducting gestures you will want to employ throughout the song by practising with the recording and in front of a mirror. Don't get hung up about what you suppose the 'correct' conducting gestures are. As long as the children know what you are asking them to do, then you must be doing it right!

What is it all about?

Singing is about doing, experiencing and feeling but, above all, it is about enjoyment.

All about warm-ups

Physical preparation

Singing is not just about using our voice box; it involves the whole of our body. We must maintain a good posture and we will use our abdomen, diaphragm and rib muscles when breathing. We use our facial muscles, our lips, tongue and teeth and, above all, our ears, which tell our bodies what we have to do to produce a beautiful, expressive sound. Our eyes and body language tell others of the feelings we wish to convey. It makes sense to prepare for this physical activity by warming up all the component parts.

Improving skills

Warm-ups are also for practising basic singing skills, in just the same way as an athlete or an instrumental player will practise their basic skills to improve their overall playing.

So, take at least five minutes to do one warm-up or two at the start of any singing session. Begin with a few body and facial flexing and relaxing exercises. Follow those with some vocal warm-ups. Constantly revisit the warm-ups and invent some of your own.

Here are a few suggestions:

But first . . .

You will probably be quite a lot taller than the children, especially those in R–Y4/P1–5. In an effort to see you, the children will stretch their necks and look up, making it difficult for them to sing. You can either direct from a chair or stand much further away from the group so that their heads are in a good position.

loosen up the body, the vocal cords and the inhibitions . . .

*   stretch each limb
*   shake out each limb
*   flick the wrists
*   tightly clench the fist or face or buttocks for ten seconds, and then relax
*   march on the spot lifting the knees up high
*   flop over like a rag doll, then slowly unfold from the bottom up, keeping the head down until last
*   stretch up as tall as possible
*   curl up as small as possible
*   roll and/or shrug the shoulders
*   give the person next to you a shoulder massage.

from the neck upwards . . .

*   tip the head gently from side to side
*   make faces to a partner (angry, sad, happy, surprised, excited, etc.) and ask them to copy
*   vulgarly chew pretend bubble gum
*   massage the face
*   squeeze the eyes tight shut for five seconds and then open them as wide as possible
*   roll the eyes
*   stretch the tongue down to the bottom of the chin and up to the tip of the nose
*   curl the tongue up
*   let the tip of the tongue go round every bit of the inside of the mouth
*   have floppy lips and make 'horse' sounds
*   make popping sounds with the lips.

from the nose downwards . . .

- make a full, slow yawn with an open mouth – let the sound come out with a sigh as the air is expelled
- breathe in slowly counting 4, hold the breath for 4, breathe out counting 4
- do as above but breathe out to a count of 6, then to 8, then 10, then 12
- do as above and breathe out to the letter F, or V or S; do not let the chest collapse when exhaling – keep it high
- take a deep breath; bend/flop over and let the body hang like a rag doll; expel air on an 'sss' sound until every little bit of it has gone; straighten the back to an upright position, raise the arms out to the side and level with the shoulders whilst taking in a deep breath; relax and breathe out as if blowing out a candle
- hum any note at a comfortable pitch and keep the sound going for several minutes by asking the children to breathe whenever they wish
- pretend to blow up a balloon
- give a great big belly laugh
- make the longest sound you can make
- make the shortest sound you can make
- make a series of short sounds.

by buzzing to find the best singing place . . .

- using both index fingers, lightly touch both sides of the nose and sing the syllable 'ing'; feel the buzz
- hum any note with loose lips and try to get the same sort of buzz.

by using your heart . . .

- make a sad sound with a sad face and gesture
- make an angry sound with an angry face and gesture
- make loving, sarcastic, surprised, happy, funny, disgusting, rude, furtive sounds and gestures.

by using your imagination . . .

- make a smacking sound
- make a popping sound
- make wet, explosive, sucking, clicking, blowing, etc., sounds.

by reaching the extremes . . .

- make the lowest sound you can make
- make the highest sound you can make
- slide the voice from top to bottom; bottom to top
- trace in the air the contour of an imaginary roller coaster, and ask the children to mirror its pathway with their voices
- vary the speed of the roller coaster; let it stop at the very top of the track, or let it crash to the bottom
- enjoy yourself; sing as if you are relaxing in a hot steamy bubble bath; no one can hear you in this resonant room because you are the only one in the house
- sing as if you are a world famous opera star
- sing as if you were the latest and most adored pop idol.

by clarifying the diction

- hum and go into one of the following vowel sounds:
  - hummm – ee (as in me)
  - hummm – e (as in bed)

- • hummm – ah (as in part)
- • hummm – oh (as in goat)
- • hummm – oo (as in toot)
- purr like a cat (roll 'r's)
- rapidly repeat individual words that are difficult to enunciate one after the other such as chocolate, lips, intimate, pop
- sing tongue twisters to the tune of the William Tell Overture, such as 'fight a frog, fight a frog, fight a frog, frog, frog', or 'crush a crisp', or 'tittle tattle'
- sing, phonetically, two consonants up and down five notes: for example, 'p and t and p and t and p' or 'k and l', etc.

There are many more exercises you can do, but these should loosen up the body, vocal cords and the children's inhibitions.

All about music, movement and dance

The importance of action in relation to thinking and learning is well recognised. We learn by 'doing'. On average we learn:

- 10 per cent of what we read
- 20 per cent of what we hear
- 30 per cent of what we see
- 50 per cent of what we see and hear
- 70 per cent of what we say
- 90 per cent of what we say and do – (Herman Ebbinhaus) because it is the doing that engages not just our mind, but our whole body in understanding and internalising feelings and concepts which are generated by musical experiences.

Some songs and music are written for dance purposes, but it is almost impossible for our bodies not to physically respond to any sort of music. It could be a toe tap to the beat, a lively dance or simply an inner stillness and intensity that allows no movement at all. Whatever the physical response to this emotional stimulus, it is almost always a pleasurable experience and one which invites repetition.

There are many ways in which movement and dance can enhance the musical development of a child.

Dance	Music	Musical elements
concentration	concentration	
movement memory	musical memory	
stillness	silence	dynamics
qualities of movement	qualities of sound	timbre
differences in energy; gross and small motor movement	differences in volume	dynamics
speed in travelling	variety in speed	tempo
movement patterning	rhythmic and melodic patterning	duration and structure
regularity of movement	pulse	duration
movement sequences	rhythmic and melodic sequences	duration and structure
repetition of movements	rhythmic and melodic repetition	duration and structure
combination of different moves and pathways	layers of sound	texture
structure of a dance	musical structure	structure
motor skills, control and co-ordination	playing instruments	
spatial awareness	awareness of phrase length	structure
focused listening to translate movement into a physical, visible form	listening skills	
interpretative skills	interpretative skills	all the elements
sensitivity and emotional response to dance	sensitivity and emotional response to music	all the elements
creativity and imagination	creativity and imagination	all the elements
timing and anticipation	timing and anticipation	rhythm
awareness of others	working with others	

Sounds of Singing

When creating a dance or movement for a song, let the words as well as the music suggest the steps and actions.

Keep the movements simple.

Rehearse until the dancers can perform as a group, i.e. as a single unit and not as several individuals.

The number one skill: breathing

This chapter offers a range of approaches for helping children to master the number one singing skill: managing breathing. Lessons 3 and 4 are entirely devoted to understanding how to breathe. They look at the role that the abdominal muscles play in deep breathing, in increasing the volume and in reaching higher notes. Attention is also paid to 'staggered breathing', an essential skill when singing long unbroken passages.

Chants are used to increase the awareness of dynamics, pitch and diction and to improve the 'ensemble', i.e. the ability of a group to sound as one. There is an opportunity to sing a song that begins quietly and finishes loudly. This demands careful listening to execute a perfectly graded crescendo throughout the piece.

Every chapter in this book focuses on one or two particular aspects of singing, and the lessons look in depth at the musical and singing skills related to those aspects. However, any song that we sing requires a multitude of skills to make it sound not merely good or even excellent, but outstanding. Chapter 1 features the first two of nine lessons in this book that are devoted to one song. All the skills that go towards creating an outstanding performance are covered in these nine lessons. The song used to illustrate how satisfying and rewarding it can be to aim for 'outstanding' is the multi-faceted 'Songs of the West'.

In this chapter, children learn about the history and background of the component songs and they sing the main melody, paying attention to posture, a 'smiley' face, and staggered breathing. An overview of the complete 'Songs of the West' project appears on page 114.

Lesson	Focus
Ebony Trousers	Humming with a buzz
	Learning to stagger breathing
	Articulating rhythmically with agility and clarity
	Performing a soundscape round in 2, 3 or 4 parts
	Singing a round in 2, 3 or 4 parts
The Termite	Listening with concentration, in order to internalise rhythmic and pitch patterns
	Working with a group
	Recognising areas for improvement
	Improving their work
You'll Never Walk Alone (1)	Adopting the correct singing posture
	Breathing deeply
	Identifying the abdominal muscles
	Chanting percussive ostinato patterns

Lesson	Focus
	Understanding how to increase the volume when singing
	Recognising the relationship between the lyrics and the expressive use of melody and dynamics
You'll Never Walk Alone (2)	Managing the breath
	Learning how to reach high notes
	Singing legato
	Paying attention to dynamics
	Recognising key consonants
Songs of the West (1)	Introducing a project on Songs of the West
	Learning about the origins of the songs
	Learning about the lyrics
Songs of the West (2)	Taking deep breaths
	Learning the melody line
	Taking quick breaths
	Singing through phrases

The number one skill: breathing

Ebony Trousers

Focus

Humming with a buzz. Learning to stagger breathing. Articulating rhythmically with agility and clarity. Performing a soundscape round in 2, 3 or 4 parts. Singing a round in 2, 3 or 4 parts.

Resources

CD 1 tracks 1, 2; song sheets 1, 2; information sheet 1.

About the song

A round from Switzerland.

Activities

Staggered breathing with a buzz-hum

Humming produces a good, unforced, well-balanced sound and helps us to 'place the sound forward' and not sing from the back of the throat. Ask the children to keep their teeth slightly apart, to rest their top lip very lightly on their bottom lip and to have both forefingers gently touching either side of their nose. Tell them to hum on any comfortable note and to feel the vibrations in their nose. Once they can feel the nose-buzz, ask them to remove their hands and see if they can feel their lips buzzing. When they need a breath, they should fade out, breathe in, then gradually fade in again. The class hum should be continuous and perfectly smooth so that nobody's breathing can be detected. Make the exercise last for at least a minute and preferably much longer.

Now do the same again, but instead of humming, ask the children to repeat the word 'Rumpf' over and over. Once again the breathing should go undetected.

The Ritti-ritti Soundscape

The Ritti-ritti Soundscape will help with articulation in the Ebony Trousers round. Play track 2 and teach the whole class, by rote, one part at a time. Observe the dynamics and other expressive elements and practise slowly until some of the more difficult phrases roll lightly off the tongue. Think about the timbre (colour) of the words, the clarity of the consonants and try to contrast the pitch of the voices for each different vocal line. Keep a steady beat by tapping claves or a wood block. When the Soundscape is rhythmically secure and really together, organise the class to say it, first in two parts, then three and finally in all four parts.

Ebony Trousers

Play the round (track 1) and if you have a balance control help the children to learn the song by listening and copying the single line of vocals. Practise the pronunciation of the Swiss German words by saying them slowly in the rhythm of the melody. When the whole round can be sung by heart, put it into parts: at first in two parts, then three and finally in all four parts.

Tricky bits

- Try to breathe only in the places marked on the song sheet.
- Stagger the breathing in the third section – Rumpf, Rumpf etc.
- Make the singing very light and bouncy and slightly staccato (detached).
- Say 'we've our' and not 'we vower'.

Observe the accent in the ritti-ritti section. Lightly pronounce 'ritti' aiming for the next accent point. When fluent, the accents can be dropped. This should help with this very tricky line.

Achievement

Can hum with a buzz. Can stagger the breathing effectively. Can articulate most or all of the phrases with clarity. Can perform a soundscape round rhythmically and with good diction. Can sing a round in 2 or 3 or 4 parts.

SONG SHEET 1

Ebony Trousers

Music by Otto Müller-Blum
English words by George Odam

4

Ebony Trousers (continued)

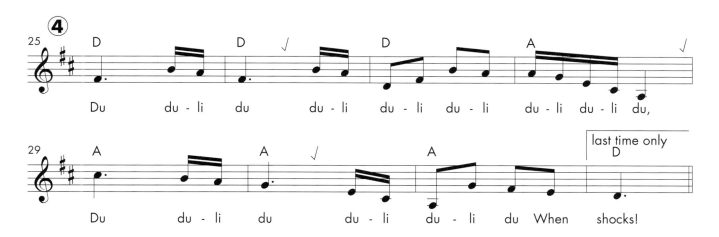

Du   du - li du   du - li   du - li du - li   du - li du - li du,

Du   du - li du   du - li   du - li du When   shocks!

last time only

Sounds of Singing

INFORMATION SHEET 1

The Ritti-ritti Soundscape

1st part	rit-ti	rit-ti	rit-ti	rit-ti	rit-ti	rit-ti	rit-ti	rit-ti	rumpf	rumpf		
	rit-ti	rit-ti	rit-ti	rit-ti	rit-ti	rit-ti	rit-ti	rit-ti	rumpf	rumpf		
2nd part	du	du-li	du	du-li	du-	li	du-	li	du-li	du		
	du	du-li	du	du-li	du-	li	du-	li	du-li	du		
3rd part	ri-	ra	ri-	ra	ri-	rit-ti	rit-ti	rit-ti	rit-ti			
	ri-	ra	ri-	ra	ri-	rit-ti	rit-ti	rit-ti				
4th part	rumpf	rumpf	rumpf	rumpf	rumpf	rumpf	rumpf	rumpf	rumpf	rumpf	rumpf	rumpf
	rumpf	rumpf	rumpf	rumpf	rumpf	rumpf	rumpf	rumpf	rumpf	rumpf	rumpf	

Each line should be repeated for as many times as you wish. Play around with the structure of the Soundscape until you have decided on its length and on a good way to begin and end.

Dynamics and other expressive elements

mf moderately loud	Rit-ti should be said very lightly, with lots of the 't' sound.
mp to *f* moderately quiet to loud	Du, du-li should be legato (smooth) with a good 'oo' sound on the 'u' vowel.
	There is a crescendo (getting louder) from the 1st to the 3rd bar and a diminuendo (getting quieter) in the 4th bar.
	Ri-ra should have rolled 'r's. Sustain the vowel sound until the beginning of the next word.
mp moderately quiet	
p quiet	Rumpf should rumble quietly in the background with a slight accent (emphasis) on the first beat of every bar.

Ebony Trousers round

This is the structure of the Ebony Trousers round sung by the children on the recording:

All   sing the first two lines in Swiss German and continue to the end of the song. Repeat the first two lines but in English.

2-bar instrumental interlude.

Group 1	sings the whole round through 3 times.
Group 2	sings the whole round through 2.75 times.
Group 3	sings the whole round through 2.5 times.
Group 4	sings the whole round through 2.25 times.

Sounds of Singing Y5–6/P6–7 © Alison Ley, Nelson Thornes Ltd, 2004

The number one skill: breathing

The Termite

Focus

Listening with concentration, in order to internalise rhythmic and pitch patterns. Working with a group. Recognising areas for improvement. Improving their work.

Resources

CD 1 tracks 3, 4; song sheet 3; two spaces to accommodate half a class in each space.

About the song

This is one of Ogden Nash's many humorous poems.

Activities

Listening to two chants

Play The Termite chant on track 3 followed by the second version on track 4. Ask the children to identify the main difference between the chants. (*Different accents on different words and different word rhythms.*)

Learning the chants

Work with the whole class. Listen and practise each chant until the children can copy the rhythms, the accents, the expression and the speed. Divide the class in two. Allocate one chant to each group and ask them to perform their chant. Make an audio or video recording of each group's performance, but do not play them the recording just yet.

Improving the chants

Ask each group to evaluate the other group's work and make suggestions for improvement.

The following questions could be useful as a guide:

- Is the whole group thinking and performing rhythmically?
- Are they all remembering to put the accents in the correct places?
- Are they all making the pitch of their voices rise and fall in the same way?
- Is there enough variation in the pitch of the voice?
- Is there any variation in the dynamics?
- Does the expression reflect the humour?
- Are they all really working their lips, tongues and teeth to pronounce the words clearly?
- Can all the consonants be heard clearly – not over-emphasised, but lightly caressed?
- Do their faces look as if they are telling a humorous tale?

Each group must now find a space, and improve their work. When both groups are satisfied with their version, make another recording (or video clip) of both groups. If the improvement is clear to see, play both the first and second recordings and ask the children to talk about the skills they had to employ in order to produce the second improved performance.

Achievement

Can internalise rhythmic and pitch patterns. Can work in a large group. Can identify areas for improvement. Can make improvements to their work

SONG SHEET 3

The Termite

Ogden Nash

Version 1
Some **pri**mal termite **knocked** on wood,
And **tas**ted it and **found** it good;
And **that** is why your **Cous**in May
Fell through the kitchen **floor** today.

Version 2
Some primal **ter**mite knocked on **wood,**
And tasted **it** and found **it** good;
And that is **why** your Cousin **May**
Fell **through** the kitchen **floor** today.

The number one skill: breathing

You'll Never Walk Alone (1)

Focus

Adopting the correct singing posture. Breathing deeply. Identifying the abdominal muscles. Chanting percussive ostinato patterns. Understanding how to increase the volume when singing. Recognising the relationship between the lyrics and the expressive use of melody and dynamics.

Resources

CD 1 tracks 5, 6, 7, 8, 9, 10; song sheet 4.

About the song

This song originally came from the stage and film musical *Carousel*, written by two Americans: Richard Rogers (music) and Oscar Hammerstein (words). The original story is partly a ghost story, and tells of the continuing love, even after death, of a man for a woman.

Activities

Re-visit 'All about singing'

Remind yourself and the children about breath management by referring to 'All about breathing' in the 'All about singing' section at the front of the book.

Some more abdominal activities

Ask the children to do the following activity – in short bursts, as too much deep breathing can make them feel faint. Play and teach the four ostinato (repeated) patterns one at a time (tracks 5–8). As they vocalise each sound, the children will need to give a little sharp pull in, on their abdominal muscles, to achieve that same energetic, percussive sound. If they put their hand on their navel, they should feel their muscles pulling in and forcing the air out of their lungs. When the sounds are punchy and rhythmically accurate, combine first two, then three and finally all four patterns together, repeating them over and over. Put in the actions and vary the dynamics as you wish.

Some children may like to create their own ostinato pattern piece by making up punchy vocal sounds that will require the abdominal muscles to be used in a similar way.

Listening to the song

Play the recording of You'll Never Walk Alone (track 10). Discuss the lyrics and the song's association with Liverpool Football Club. Point out that the melody reflects the lyrics by starting low and gradually rising in pitch and volume all through the song with the highest and loudest note (the climax of the song) coming in the last phrase on the very important word 'never'. Allow the children to absorb the song by playing the recording during registration, break times, and, when appropriate, as background music in class.

How to crescendo

To sing loudly, and to reach high notes without forcing the voice, the children must adopt a good singing posture and use their abdominal muscles. Play track 9 and hear how the singer slowly increases the volume of her hum. To do this the children should take in a 'drink' of air that goes right down low, as if their tummy is a tank of air, and, to a count of 8 or 12, gradually increase the volume by slowly pulling in their abdominal muscles to push out the air. Choose any starting note and change the sound to 'ah' or 'oo' or whatever, but do not allow the volume to increase to an unpleasant forced shouting sound. The more you re-visit all these exercises, the better the children's understanding and ability will become.

In lesson 4, the children will sing You'll Never Walk Alone, applying all the above singing techniques.

Achievement

Can adopt the correct singing posture. Can breathe deeply. Can identify abdominal muscles. Can chant rhythmically using abdominal muscles. Can understand how to increase the volume when singing. Can relate lyrics to the melodic line and dynamics.

SONG SHEET 4

Vocal Ostinato Patterns

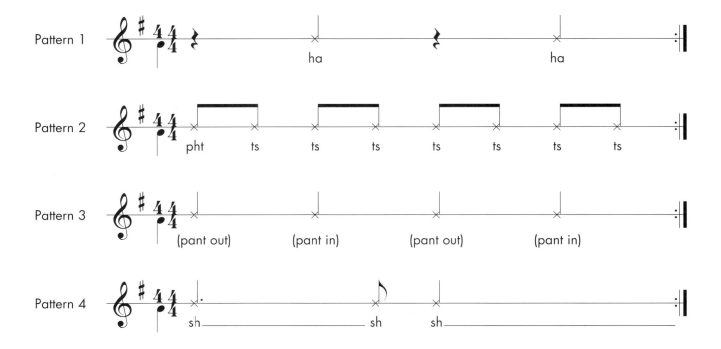

Helpful actions to perform in the same rhythms as the ostinato patterns:

Pattern 1
- Put hands in front of you, keeping elbows bent, palms facing the ceiling. Each time you say 'ha', pretend you are lifting a heavy weight and move your hands upwards.

Pattern 2
- With each sound, pull your navel in towards your backbone.

Pattern 3
- Pant like a dog with your tongue hanging out.

Pattern 4
- Make potato fists. Hold one above the other. Keep top fist still and punch the bottom one upwards into the top one.

The number one skill: breathing

Lesson 4

You'll Never Walk Alone (2)

Focus

Managing the breath. Learning how to reach high notes. Singing legato. Paying attention to dynamics. Recognising key consonants.

Resources

CD 1 track 10; song sheets 5, 6; a projector or board on which to display the song.

About the song

This song originally came from the stage and film musical *Carousel*, written by two Americans: Richard Rodgers (music) and Oscar Hammerstein (words). The original story is partly a ghost story, and tells of the continuing love, even after death, of a man for a woman.

Activities

It is advisable to have covered Chapter 1 lesson 3 before embarking on this lesson and to revise the section on 'Posture' on page xiii.

Blow out the candles

Ask the children to stand with a good singing posture, to spread the fingers of one hand and to place it about 20cm in front of their face. They should imagine that each finger is a lighted candle which has to be extinguished, one at time, with a quick, forceful stream of air. They should give a sharp inward pull with their abdominal muscles to push the air out of their lungs and they should be able to feel the cold air on the tip of each individual finger.

Hum whole phrases

Display the song and ask the children to hum the melody with the recording, observing all breath marks. Remind them to breathe into the bottom of their lungs taking in just the right amount of breath for each phrase.

When the high notes appear, ask the children:

- to ensure they take in enough breath at the beginning of the phrase
- to open their mouths from top to bottom
- not to point their heads upwards
- to give a little extra pull in with their abdominal muscles to 'support' the high notes
- not to force their voices by trying to sing excessively loudly.

Adding the words and expression

Ask the children to:

- fix their eyes on the conductor, and be ready to say 'wh' at the beginning of the first word.
- sing legato (smoothly) by maintaining long vowel sounds and lightly tucking the following consonant in at the very last moment.
- lightly weight some consonants, for dramatic effect, e.g. **d**ark, **g**olden, **n**ever.
- try not to run the final consonant of a word into the initial vowel of the next word: e.g. 'When you' and not 'Whe-new'; 'head up' and not 'hea-dup'; 'walk on' and not 'war-kon', etc. Put a mini gap between the two words and make a clean vowel sound at the beginning of the second word.
- pay great attention to the expression and the dynamics. Start the song quietly and let each new phrase grow in volume just a little bit more than the previous one.
- find the focal point of each individual phrase, sing towards that focal point and give each phrase a musical shape of its own.

Achievement

Can breathe in phrase lengths. Can reach the high notes. Can sing legato. Can sing a 'managed' crescendo. Can identify the key consonants. Can sing with attention to expression and dynamics.

SONG SHEET 5

You'll Never Walk Alone

Words by Oscar Hammerstein II
Music by Richard Rodgers

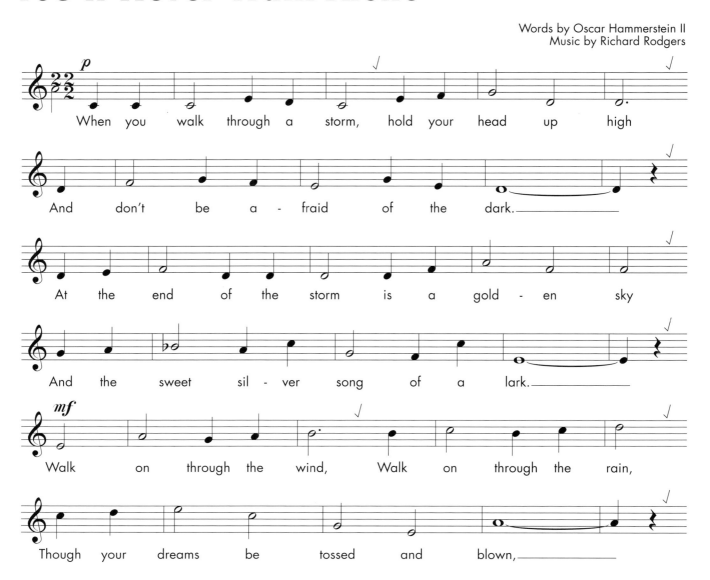

You'll Never Walk Alone (continued)

Walk on, walk on, with hope in your heart,

And you'll nev - er walk a - lone, _____

You'll nev - er walk a - lone! _____

The number one skill: breathing

Lesson 5

Songs of the West (1)

Focus

Introducing a project on Songs of the West. Learning about the origins of the songs. Learning about the lyrics.

Resources

CD 1 tracks 11, 12, 13, 14; song sheets 7, 8.

About the song

Three traditional American folksongs. Railroad men and hobos (vagrants and travelling workers) were the heroes of many 1930s and 1940s American folk songs. The railroad itself was an important symbol to Americans and was more than just a means of transport – it also meant freedom and opportunity.

Activities

Understanding the lyrics

Three songs are combined in Songs of the West: Rock Island Line, Midnight Special and Worried Man. Discuss the origins and lyrics of each song.

Rock Island Line

The Rock Island Railway Line was built between 1851 and 1854 and connected Chicago to Rock Island on the Mississippi River in Illinois.

Kelly Pace, a prisoner in Arkansas, wrote this song in around 1934. Huddie 'Leadbelly' Ledbetter, the black American folk singer (died 1949), made a phonograph recording of the song. In 1955, Lonnie Donegan heard the recording and made his own arrangement of the song for guitar, bass and washboard. That song was the start of the 'skiffle' craze that swept across Britain and the USA (see Chapter 7 lesson 4).

The original words tell of a train driver on the Rock Island Line, who fools the tollgate keeper into thinking that he had livestock on board, because there was no toll on livestock. As with all folksongs, the words change over the years and there are now several different versions of this song. In this version the refrain includes 'got to ride it like you find it', whereas another has 'got to ride it like you flying'. How might these changes have occurred? (*Probably because songs were learned aurally and words misheard.*)

Midnight Special

This traditional American folksong was collected from a Texas jail in around 1933. The lyrics used in this version are those of the refrain. In the original verses a black prisoner despairs at how easy it is for black southerners to be slung into jail. He sings of his hard monotonous life. He sees the headlight of the cross-continent train boring through the night past his prison. He dreams that his sweetheart is coming with his pardon and yearns for his freedom.

Worried Man

This is a traditional Hillbilly song. Hillbillies lived simple lives in the Appalachian mountain regions of the south-eastern United States.

A man lay down to sleep by the river and awoke with 21 links of chain around his leg. For some awful crime he had committed in the past, he was sentenced to work for 21 years on the Rock Island Line, and had to watch the one he loved pass by on a 16-coach train.

Putting it all together

Finally, listen to the complete Songs of the West (track 14). Discuss why the arranger might have chosen to combine the three songs. What do they have in common? How does the music reflect the meaning of the lyrics?

Achievement

Can appreciate the origins and lyrics of the songs.

Rock Island Line

Traditional, arranged by Brian Ley

Refrain
Oh the Rock Island Line is a mighty good road,
Well the Rock Island Line is the road to ride,
Oh the Rock Island Line is a might good road,
If you want to ride it, got to ride it like you find it,
Get your ticket at the station on the Rock Island Line.

Verse 1
Train's comin' down the track, runnin' real well,
Blowin' the whistle and ringin' the bell.

Refrain
Oh the Rock Island Line...

Verse 2
Train left St Louis at quarter to nine,
Got to Fort Worth for dinner time.

Refrain
Oh the Rock Island Line...

Midnight Special

Traditional, arranged by Brian Ley

Let the Midnight Special shine its light on me,
Let the Midnight Special shine its ever-lovin' light on me.
(These lines are repeated throughout the song.)

SONG SHEET 8

Worried Man

Traditional, arranged by Brian Ley

It takes a worried man to sing a worried song,
It takes a worried man to sing a worried song,
It takes a worried man to sing a worried song,
I'm worried now, but I won't be worried long.

The train I ride is sixteen coaches long,
The train I ride is sixteen coaches long,
The train I ride is sixteen coaches long,
But the one I love was on that train and gone.

It takes a worried man to sing a worried song,
It takes a worried man to sing a worried song,
It takes a worried man to sing a worried song,
I'm worried now, but I won't be worried long.

          Sounds of Singing Y5–6/P6–7 © Alison Ley, Nelson Thornes Ltd, 2004

The number one skill: breathing

Songs of the West (2)

Focus

Taking deep breaths. Learning the melody line. Taking quick breaths. Singing through phrases.

Resources

CD 1 tracks 15, 16; song sheets 9, 10, 11, 12, 13 (12 and 13 optional).

About the song

Three traditional American folk songs.

It is advisable to have completed Chapter 1 lesson 5 before embarking upon this one.

Activities

Learning the melody

Play the song recording (all three sections) through several times until the children are familiar with the melody and can join in. If you have a balance control you can use track 15 to play the vocal melody and instrumental accompaniment, without the distraction of the vocal harmonies.

Taking a sip of air

Play track 16. Ask the children to explain the difference between the four different versions of the breathing exercise. (*The time taken for the initial intake of breath is progressively reduced.*) In the refrain of Rock Island Line, there is little time to breathe, and quick breaths have to be snatched. This exercise is for practising that skill – ask the children to try it. Breathing should still be low but only a small amount of air is inhaled.

Singing whole phrases

Encourage the children not to break the flow of the melodic line, but to keep the momentum of the song going by breathing deeply and by taking in the right amount of air for each whole phrase. The breathing points are marked on the song sheet. Quick breaths are essential in Rock Island Line. Remind the children to keep a smiley face (see All about singing, page xiii) and to maintain a good posture so that they can convey the buoyant, upbeat mood of these songs.

Achievement

Can recognise how to take low, deep breaths. Can take quick 'top-up' breaths. Can take in enough air to sing a whole phrase.

SONG SHEET 9

Rock Island Line

Traditional
arranged by Brian Ley

Sounds of Singing Y5–6/P6–7 © Alison Ley, Nelson Thornes Ltd, 2004

SONG SHEET 10

Midnight Special

Traditional
arranged by Brian Ley

SONG SHEET 11

Midnight Special (continued)

Sounds of Singing Y5–6/P6–7 © Alison Ley, Nelson Thornes Ltd, 2004

SONG SHEET 12

Worried Man

Traditional
arranged by Brian Ley

SONG SHEET 13

Worried Man (continued)

Sounds of Singing Y5–6/P6–7 © Alison Ley, Nelson Thornes Ltd, 2004

Beautiful precision

This chapter is all about improving a number of vocal techniques, including staccato (detached) and legato (smooth) singing, diction, accurate intonation (pitch) and tonal quality. It also looks into the reasons why these techniques are important and at the enormous difference that mastering these skills makes, to the quality of both the singing and the final performance of a song.

There are two rounds, one of them in Latin. Each round is recorded twice. The first recording has the vocals on one track and the backing on the second track. The second recording has the first melody line and the backing on one track, and two remaining parts are sung as a round with the backing on the other track.

One of the main ways to acquire a good blend and a good tonal quality is for everyone to sing the same vowel sound. The recording of the Latin round is an excellent example of this and subsequent exercises provide an opportunity to practise and to understand the importance of singing pure vowels. Consonants, however, are not neglected, and are used on more than one occasion to create special effects.

There are several opportunities to improve the accurate pitching of notes. These include concentrated listening activities in order to internalise pitches (hearing the sound in one's head) before they are actually sung.

Understanding how both the music and the words determine the setting and mood of a song is examined in detail. This understanding is essential if any song is to be performed with feeling and expression.

Lesson	Focus
The Coffee Round	Identifying musical features
	Singing legato and staccato
	Singing in tune
	Improving diction
	Singing unaccompanied
	Singing a three-part round
Syntax Error	Recognising and singing staccato and legato
	Singing melodic leaps in tune
	Understanding how musical features, techniques and diction create the mood and feeling of a song
	Adding movement in the mood of the song
Dona Nobis Pacem	Singing pure vowels
	Singing in tune
	Breathing unanimously
	Singing sensitively and expressively
	Holding a vocal part whilst maintaining all the above skills

Lesson	Focus
Songs of the West (3)	Identifying and performing a different accent
	Inventing and performing a patter-sentence
	Evaluating their own progress
	Achieving accuracy, precision and clarity of diction

Beautiful precision

The Coffee Round

Focus

Identifying musical features. Singing legato and staccato. Singing in tune. Improving diction. Singing unaccompanied. Singing a three-part round.

Resources

CD 1 tracks 26, 27, 28, 29; song sheet 14.

About the song

This is a traditional round.

Activities

Identifying musical features

Play The Coffee Round three times (track 26). Focus the children's listening by asking them questions each time the round is heard. What happens to children who drink coffee? (*It makes them skin and bone.*) What should they drink instead? (*Tea.*) What do they notice about the way the first six notes are sung? (*They are sung staccato – i.e. short, detached.*) What is the main instrument that plays the accompaniment? (*Accordian.*) How many parts are there in the round? (*Three parts.*)

Tuning in

Play the warm-up exercise on track 28. Ask the children to copy the phrase, singing quietly. Tell them to listen very carefully so that they can pitch the notes accurately. There is a difficult leap at the end of the phrase (C^1 to C) which may need extra practice. Now play track 29 (the same phrase sung staccato). Ask the children to sing this staccato phrase giving it some extra energy by slightly pulling in the abdominal muscles with each note that is sung.

Learning by heart

Play The Coffee Round again and ask the children to join in with the melody until they have learnt it by heart. If you have a balance control, use track 27 (split vocals) to isolate the melody and backing on its own (i.e. not in a round). Ask the children if they can hear where the first three and the last three notes of the warm-up exercise can be found. (*The first bar, 'C – O – F', and the last bar, 'cup of tea'.*) Now ask if they know where the middle three notes can be found. (*Beginning of the second line, 'children should'.*)

As soon as possible, sing the melody unaccompanied (without the recording). Help the children to:

- sing the first two bars staccato. Make the last line legato (smooth).
- give the round a dance-like feel to it by slightly emphasising the first beat of every bar.
- pronounce the 'n' on the words 'than', 'alone', 'skin' and 'bone'.
- roll the 'r' in 'drink'.
- take little breaths after 'E', 'alone', and 'far'.
- sing the last line in one breath by using their abdominal muscles to push that extra bit of air out of their lungs.

In parts

Divide the class in two and sing the song as a two-part round. It is best to sing without the recording, as both you and the children will hear when/if any mistakes occur. Still keep the singing light and bouncy; not loud. Graduate to a three-part round, perhaps adding the recorded accompaniment at this stage.

Achievement

Can recognise some musical features. Can sing legato and staccato. Can sing with good intonation. Can hear how to improve diction. Can sing in tune, unaccompanied. Can hold a vocal part.

SONG SHEET 14

The Coffee Round

Traditional round

C - O - F - F - E - E   cof - fee's   much   strong - er   than   tea.

Child - ren   should   leave   it   a - lone   for   it   makes   them   skin   and   bone.

Bet - ter   by   far   to   drink   a   cup   of   tea.

Sounds of Singing Y5–6/P6–7 © Alison Ley, Nelson Thornes Ltd, 2004

Beautiful precision

Syntax Error

Focus

Recognising and singing staccato and legato. Singing melodic leaps in tune. Understanding how musical features, techniques and diction create the mood and feeling of a song. Adding movement in the mood of the song.

Resources

CD 1 tracks 30, 31; song sheets 15, 16.

About the song

This is a contemporary Australian song that is applicable to children (and parents) all over the world.

Activities

Staccato, legato and long notes

Play Syntax Error (track 30). Point out that the notes of the melody are detached from one another. Ask the children to find the one exception where they are joined together – legato singing. ('LOAD JUNIOR JUMPMAN'.) Then ask them to find the only three long notes in the song, ('LOADING, READY', and on the last word of the refrain, 'now'.)

Making perfect jumps

The phrases 'Jump out of bed' and 'Butter some toast' both have big leaps in the melody line, which can be difficult to pitch accurately. The phrase 'Play with my computer' also has leaps where the difficulty lies in pitching the notes at that fast tempo. Ask the children to listen very carefully to the warm-up exercise (track 31), which incorporates these leaps. It is sung very slowly so that they can internalise and remember the note patterns. Ask them to copy the singer, to think the notes in their head before they sing them and then pitch their voice right in the middle of each note. You will be surprised at the improvement the children will make if they think carefully about what they are doing.

Mood, feelings and texture

Discuss with the children why the melodic jumps and the staccato singing create the right mood for this song. (*The melodic jumps reflect the 'Jumpman' game; the staccato singing reflects the tap-tap of the computer keys; there is much repetition in the melody line reflecting the mechanical nature of the activity.*) Ask them to decide which are the key words that portray the setting and mood of the song. ('*Play with my computer*' *because it is the synthesis of the song.*)

Putting it all together

To add to the mood and the feeling of the song, make the words very precise and clear. Exaggerate and 'spit' out the consonants. When singing notes at the same pitch or descending in steps, it is easy to sing flat (underneath the note), so remind the children to take in enough air for the last line of the refrain. They may like to add some 'break-dance' movements or other tight, jerky moves to go with this song.

Achievement

Can recognise and sing staccato and legato. Can internalise large leaps and sing in tune. Can understand how a 'mood' is created. Can create movement to enhance the mood of a song.

SONG SHEET 15

Syntax Error

Words and music by Peter Combe

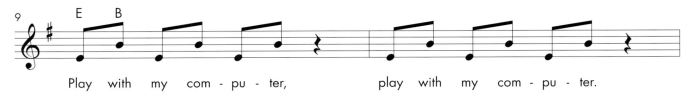

2   Insert the disc, type in 'LOAD
    JUNIOR JUMPMAN', press the return.
    Screen says 'SEARCHING FOR JUNIOR JUMPMAN'.
    'LOADING. READY'.
    Play with my computer, play with my computer.

Syntax Error (continued)

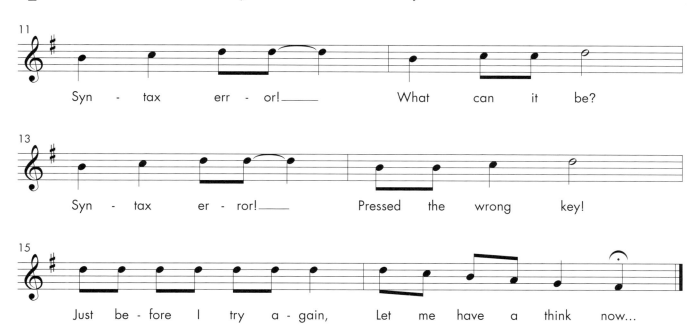

Syn - tax err - or!_____ What can it be?

Syn - tax er - ror!_____ Pressed the wrong key!

Just be - fore I try a - gain, Let me have a think now...

3   My Dad doesn't know a byte from a bite.
    My Mum, I'm afraid, isn't much better.
    They don't understand, they don't know where it's at.
    What can you do with parents like that,
    Who play with my computer, play with my computer?

    Syntax error! What can it be?
    Syntax error! Pressed the wrong key!

CHAPTER 2

Beautiful precision

Lesson 3

Dona Nobis Pacem

Focus

Singing pure vowels. Singing in tune. Breathing unanimously. Singing sensitively and expressively. Holding a part whilst maintaining all the above skills.

Resources

CD 1 tracks 32, 33, 34; song sheet 17.

About the song

This is a traditional round. The Latin words 'dona nobis pacem' mean 'give us peace'.

The singing skills that all combine to make the recorded version of this round sound so beautiful are the unanimity of the pure Latin vowels, the accurate intonation (tuning), the unanimous breathing and the legato line.

Activities

Unanimity of vowels

- Dona and nobis as in 'phone' or 'cone' – not as in 'gone' or 'con'.
- Nobis as in peace or fleece – not as in 'kiss' or 'this'.
- Dona and pacem as in a bright sounding '**ah**' – not dull and flat sounding, and not as in 'pack' or 'stack'.
- Pacem as in 'ever' or 'weather' – not a soft schwa as in 'taken' or 'spoken'.

Ask the children to say the Latin words with the consistent vowel pronunciation and then copy the warm-up exercise (track 32), singing quietly so that they can hear themselves and others.

Singing the song

Use the recording to help the children to learn the song. If your CD player has a balance control you have the options of isolating the vocal parts from the instrumentals (track 33) and also listening to the melody alone (i.e. not in a round, as on track 34).

Accurate intonation

The intonation will be helped if the children remember to breathe correctly. (See All about breathing, page xiii.) Watch out for the following places where the pitch could drop:

- Any sequence of notes that moves down in steps.
- The jumps in the first two bars, also in the fifth bar from the end, and in the penultimate bar.
- Any note that is repeated at the same pitch.

Unanimity of breathing, dynamics and expression

Shorten the last note of each phrase by one beat (a crotchet) to allow the children time to take sufficient breath. Shape each phrase by adhering to the dynamics shown on the song sheet. Watch out for the following tricky bits:

- Lighten the second syllable of 'pacem'.
- Gently crescendo (get louder) at the beginning of lines two and three.
- Do not rush the quicker notes (quavers).

Follow all the hairpin $<$ $>$, accent f and breath marks. Do not go over the top; at no time does the singing need to be very loud.

- Sing legato: i.e. sing sustained, smooth phrases.

In a round

Sing the song as a round only when the skills are memorised and the quality of singing is good. It is better for the children to sing really well in unison than to sing in a round and give a mediocre performance.

Achievement

Can hear and sing pure vowels. Can pitch notes accurately. Can breathe with others. Can sing sensitively and expressively. Can hold a vocal part whilst maintaining the above skills.

Dona Nobis Pacem

CHAPTER 2

Beautiful precision

Lesson 4

Songs of the West (3)

Focus

Identifying and performing a different accent. Inventing and performing a patter-sentence. Evaluating their own progress. Achieving accuracy, precision and clarity of diction.

Resources

CD 1 tracks 14, 15, 17; song sheets 9–13 (on pages 18–22), 18.

About the song

Three traditional American folk songs. See Chapter 1 lesson 5.

Activities

Before attempting this lesson, you must have completed Chapter 1 Lesson 5.

The mid-Atlantic accent

Play Songs of the West (split vocals version, track 15) and ask the children to pick out any words or phrases which have an American-style accent ('*mighty*', '*If you want to ride it*', '*lovin*', '*shine its light on*', *etc.*) If you have a balance control you can hear the words more clearly by isolating the vocal melody line. Go over the words and agree on a unified pronunciation. Rehearse the songs with this more relaxed style of articulation.

Patter verse

(A patter song is a comic song, often used in opera, in which the words are sung extremely fast.)

Copy or project song sheet 14 or write the words on the board. Ask the class to listen to the patter warm-up (track 17) and then recite the nonsense verse. Both the words and the rhythm are taken from Songs of the West. Keeping the 'American' accent they should say it quietly, all in one breath, busily working their lips, tongue, teeth and face muscles and make it sound like the 'clackety clack' of a train. Now ask the children to work with a partner and to make up their own nonsense verse in the same rhythm, using words from the song. The sentence can be any length, but must be said in one breath.

Practising the patter verse

Ask for volunteers to perform their verse. Choose four different verses and write them on the board. Divide the class into four groups allocating one verse to each group. Appoint the verse authors to be group leaders. Ask them to help their group to say their sentence at four different speeds: lento (slow), presto (fast), accelerando (slow then getter faster), rallentando (fast then getting slower). They must work on the accuracy and tightness of the rhythm and the clarity of the words. Allow the children to record their performances and to appraise their own work. They should continue to practise and record their efforts until they are satisfied with their achievements.

Attack and tempo

Sing the Songs of the West with the backing track (track 14). Ask the children to breathe with you at the beginning of each song. This should ensure that everyone starts together. In Rock Island Line, don't let the tempo (speed) drag in the refrain and do not let the children swallow the first two words of the first four phrases ('*Oh the*', '*Well the*', '*Oh the*', '*If you*'.)

Achievement

Can identify the American-style accent. Can invent a patter verse. Can work with a group and evaluate their progress. Can chant and sing with accuracy, precision and clarity in a more relaxed style of articulation.

Songs of the West Patter

Let the good shine on the Special
Take a ride and if you want it
Get a ticket at St Louis
But before the station whistle
You must ring the bell and fly it
Where the lovin' light will down it
To a worried man who sings it
On the Midnight train now flyin'
Me to see the one I love.

ABOUT CHAPTER 3

Feel and sing the rhythm

The time signature (the number like a fraction at the beginning of each song) indicates the metre of the song – the number of beats in a bar, and what kind of beats they are. In conventional notation $\frac{3}{4}$ means there are three crotchets in a bar. Throughout this book, the time signatures are expressed like this $\frac{3}{\downarrow}$ in order to help children understand that the top number tells us the number of beats in a bar, and the bottom number tell us what type of beats they are. The steady 'strong, weak, weak' basic pulse within each bar is known as the 'metre', whilst 'rhythm' is defined as the actual time-values of the notes heard within the bar.

This chapter focuses on the importance of singing rhythmically. That might mean singing exactly as the rhythm is written or interpreting the notation in a looser style appropriate to a particular song, where the rhythm can only be felt and not precisely notated.

The activities include recognising and clapping the 'off' beat and other syncopated rhythms, feeling the subtleties of the rhythm in a particular style of music, and understanding and 'doing' the difference between pulse/steady beat, metre and rhythm.

There are four two-part songs. The second part is always simple but if you feel that your children are not ready for two-part singing, aim for outstanding unison singing with good-quality tuning, blend and tone.

Once again breathing is revised, this time in order to work on keeping chromatic passages (notes that move very closely in step) in tune and as a technique to use when powerful singing is required.

There is an opportunity to do some scat singing – improvising and interpolating nonsense words and syllables over the harmonies of a song.

This whole chapter would not make sense unless every muscle in our bodies could feel and internalise the beat and rhythms, so movement is as much a part of these songs as is the singing.

Lesson	Focus
Everybody's Got a	Clapping on the 'off' beat
Little Rhythm	Feeling and singing the syncopated rhythm
	Singing in a pop style
Silver Moon	Understanding the importance of feeling the metre and rhythm of a song
	Singing a second part
	Singing in tune
	Moving in performance
Work-a-day Mornin' blues	Learning about the blues
	Listening to and understanding improvisation
	Listening to scat singing
	Learning to sing scat
	Improvising rhythms

Lesson	Focus
Songs of the West (4)	Recognising and understanding how 'popular' (jazz, swing, pop and rock) rhythms are written and performed
	Recognising a canon
	Learning a harmony part
	Putting two parts together
Good News	Learning about spirituals and gospel singing
	Singing in two parts
	Singing with power and control
	Moving and performing in the gospel style

CHAPTER 3

Feel and sing the rhythm

Lesson 1

Everybody's Got a Little Rhythm

Focus

Clapping on the 'off' beat. Feeling and singing the syncopated rhythm. Singing in a pop style.

Resources

CD 2 tracks 1, 2, 3, 4; song sheet 19.

About the song

A song that focuses on syncopated rhythm. The structure of this song as recorded is:

A (refrain)
B (verse 1)
A (refrain)
B* (verse 2)
A (refrain)
A & B (refrain and verse 1 simultaneously)
A & B* (refrain and verse 2 simultaneously)
coda (ending).

Activities

The 'off' beat

Invite the children to hold one hand open with the palm facing downwards, about 20cm above their lap. With their other hand they should make a fist. Play Everybody's Got a Little Rhythm (track 1) and ask them to keep a steady beat by alternately touching their thigh and then slamming into the palm of their hand with the clenched fist (thigh slam thigh slam). When this pattern is fluent, ask them to make a small downward movement on the strong beat instead of actually touching their thigh. The sound that is left (slam) is being heard on the weaker 'off beat'.

Syncopated rhythms

When a strong emphasis is placed on a weak beat, it is known as syncopation. This song is full of syncopated rhythms. In popular music it is not always possible to write down the exact notation for the jazzy rhythms that are required. Rhythm has to be 'felt' first. Play the song again and tell the children that the very first rhythm of the piece is not as it is written, but it is being sung as it is 'felt'. However, the trickiest rhythm to get everyone singing and feeling correctly occurs in the first two notes of every bar of the verse. Ask the children to listen carefully to the singer on Rhythm Warm-up (track 3) as she says and drums this rhythm with a steady beat going on in the background. Then ask them to whisper the words with the recording copying the rhythm exactly. Next ask them to clap the word rhythm with the whisper.

Singing with attitude

This song needs to be sung enthusiastically and in a relaxed pop kind of style. However, if the syncopated rhythm is not tight and it is not 'felt', then the song loses its momentum as well as its appeal. Ask the children to listen to the singer on track 4; she is singing the rhythms too straight and the song is dull and ordinary. Ask the children to put some 'punch' into their voices without singing in a shouting voice. As they are singing, some children may be able to click their fingers on the 'off' beat to add to the sense of syncopation.

Achievement

Can clap on the 'off' beat. Can feel and sing syncopated rhythms. Can sing in a pop style.

Everybody's Got a Little Rhythm

Words and music by Peter Combe

CHAPTER 3

Feel and sing the rhythm

Lesson 2

Silver Moon

Focus

Understanding the importance of feeling the metre and rhythm of a song. Singing a second part. Singing in tune. Moving in performance.

Resources

CD 2 track 5; song sheets 20, 21.

About the song

An anonymous, catchy song.

Activities

Listening and thinking musically

Play Silver Moon (track 5). Ask the children to listen to the song and discuss with them any interesting musical features. (*Relaxed style of singing; slightly jazzy feel with syncopated rhythms (bars 3, 7, 15) and 'blue' notes (flattened notes such as B♭ in bar 12); a good strong beat; in two parts; the harmony part is higher in pitch than the melody line.*)

Feeling and doing the steady beat/metre/pulse

(Please refer to About Chapter 3 on page 34 for an explanation of beat, metre, pulse, rhythm and time signatures.)

The best way to feel any beat, metre or pulse, is to move to it, so play track 5 again and ask the children to:

* clap on the first beat of every bar, and to make a small, relaxed, 'hammer tapping' type of movement, in the air, with alternate hands and forearms, for the remaining three beats of each bar.
* walk the pulse, clapping their hands on the strong first beat of every bar.
* sing the melody, walk the pulse and clap their hands.
* sing the melody, walk the pulse, clap their hands, and change the direction in which they are walking at the end of each phrase (after every four bars).

Tuning the top part

Listen to track 5. Use the balance control to play the harmony part (top line of music) only. This melodic line uses very few notes, but there is a danger of singing it flat because:

* the harmony part is sung like a 'descant' and the notes feel high, even though they are not.
* most of the notes move chromatically (in very close steps) and it is always difficult to tune chromatic passages.
* phrases that contain repeated notes or long notes tend to sag (drop in pitch) as the air supply diminishes.

If the pitch does drop, ask the children to stand, and to adopt a good singing posture. Remind them about breathing deeply and working hard with their abdominal muscles. Practise some of the energising and breathing exercises in 'All about warm-ups' (page xviii) and revise the breathing exercises in Chapter 1, lessons 3 and 4. When practising, the children will hear what they are singing if they hum and sing the part quietly. Invite those children who are happy with their performance to sing the upper part whilst the rest of the class sings the main tune.

Presenting and performing

Encourage the children to find some very simple movements that swing along with this song just so that they do not all stand stiffly and to attention.

Achievement

Can understand about metre and rhythm. Can move to the metre. Can sing a second part. Can sing in tune. Can give a good performance.

SONG SHEET 20

Silver Moon

Anon.

SONG SHEET 21

Silver Moon (continued)

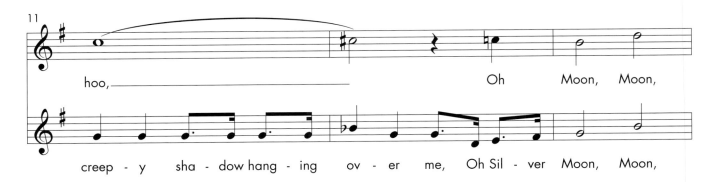

hoo, _____ Oh Moon, Moon,

creep - y sha - dow hang - ing ov - er me, Oh Sil - ver Moon, Moon,

bright and shin - y moon, Won't you please shine down on me?

bright and shin - y moon, Won't you please shine down on me?

Feel and sing the rhythm

Lesson 3

Work-a-day Mornin' Blues

Focus

Learning about the blues. Listening to and understanding improvisation. Listening to scat singing. Learning to sing scat. Improvising rhythms.

Resources

CD 2 tracks 6, 7; a large space, if possible (optional); song sheet 22.

About the song

Blues music is a fusion of African music and European harmonies, which were taken from hymn tunes sung by the slaves in the southern states of America. These songs usually expressed the misery of slavery or an unhappy love affair.

Blues history

Play track 6 several times, both as background music and as focused listening. Explain to the children that blues music now comes under the generic term of 'jazz'. Blues songs are usually 12 bars long, and they all have the same harmonic structure. 'Blue notes' are notes that have been flattened to give a bluesy feel. These are marked on the song sheet.

Harmonica improvisation

If you have a balance control, play just the backing track and focus the children's listening on the harmonica playing. Ask them to identify when the harmonica plays (*mostly at the end of every line and in-between the verses*) and what it plays (*improvised phrases, and snatches of phrases, that mix and match with the rest of the song*). Explain that improvisation is the essence of jazz music.

Listening and performing scat singing

Play track 7 and ask the children to listen to the singer as she sings along with the recording. Ask them to describe what she is singing. (*She is improvising and interpolating nonsense words and syllables in the blues song. This is known as scat singing.*)

Now play track 6 again (the non-scat version of the song) and ask the children to imagine that they are walking in a favourite place. If there is space they can really move around. They are feeling good and are playing Work-a-day Mornin' Blues on their personal stereo. Nobody is within hearing distance so they decide to sing along with the music using different words, different syllables, different notes, different sounds, etc. that will mix and match with the singer on the recording. If they sing too loudly, they won't be able to hear the recording so tell them to put one finger in one ear and they should be able to sing quietly *and* hear themselves more clearly into the bargain. They do not need to sing all the time – they can leave gaps. Do this several times and on several different occasions, until they begin to feel comfortable with their improvisations.

If you have an electronic keyboard, create a blues backing by selecting a jazz rhythm style and play a left-hand single-finger accompaniment to the following blues chord sequence: D D D D, G G D D, A_7 A_7 D D. Repeat the above scat-singing activity with the class using this new backing track.

For those children who find scat singing difficult, ask them to improvise (by lightly clapping) some jazzy rhythm patterns at the end of the lines and in between the verses.

Achievement

Can understand improvisation and scat singing. Can sing scat. Can improvise jazzy rhythm patterns.

SONG SHEET 22

Workaday Mornin' Blues

Music by Sol Berkowitz
Words by Rosemary Jacques

Feel and sing the rhythm

Songs of the West (4)

Focus

Recognising and understanding how 'popular' (jazz, swing, pop and rock) rhythms are written and performed. Recognising a canon. Learning a harmony part. Putting two parts together.

Resources

CD 1 tracks 11, 19, 20; song sheets 9, 10, 11 (pages 18–20).

About the song

Three traditional American folk songs. See Chapter 1 lesson 5.

Activities

Swinging the rhythm

Play both the original (CD 1, track 11) and 'new' (track 19) recordings of Rock Island Line. Ask the children what is different about the rhythms on the original recording and the new version. (*The new version is sung straight – i.e. exactly as the rhythm is written.*) Play both recordings again and ask the children to whisper the words along with each one. Ask them what the difference feels like. What does it do to the mood and character of the song? (*The original version changes the written rhythm into the more relaxed jazzy style. Sung straight, the song loses its meaning, its style and its appeal.*) Explain that in jazz, rhythm and blues, rock, swing music, and so on, there are no written notes that equate with the complexity of such rhythms. Performers get to know, by experience, what rhythms to play in different styles of music. There are many such examples in all types of music where instructions cannot be written down but the performer knows that he or she has to play music in a certain style or use a certain chord structure, or whatever.

Imitating rhythms

Ask the children in what way they think the rhythms of Rock Island Line reflect the words. (*The 'tick-a-tack-a' rhythm is similar to the clickety-clack rhythm of a train.*)

Singing in canon

Play Midnight Special (track 20) and teach the children the second part. If you have a balance control you can remove the first part in order to hear the the second and third parts more clearly. The second part is the same as the main tune except for 'shine its light on me'. The first half of the second part, (bars 10 to 17) is repeated exactly in bars 18 to 25. When one part imitates another part, it is called canonic imitation.

Putting the parts together

When the second part is really secure ask the class to sing it with the melody line of the recording. Now divide the class in two and sing both parts together. Never be tempted to invite failure by putting parts together before both individual parts are really secure and preferably known by heart. Listen for the long notes on the words 'special' and 'me', but give the children time to breathe deeply after the word 'me'. Note that there is no breath mark after the word 'special'. Keep the diction relaxed, but ensure that the song moves along in a lively and rhythmic manner.

Achievement

Can understand and recognise the difference between the popular style rhythms and their performance. Can identify a canon. Can sing a second part.

CHAPTER 3

Feel and sing the rhythm

Lesson 5

Good News

Focus

Learning about spirituals and gospel singing. Singing in two parts. Singing with power and control. Moving and performing in the gospel style.

Resources

CD 2 tracks 8, 9; song sheet 23, 24.

About the song

This is a traditional spiritual, sung in the gospel style.

Activities

About spirituals and gospel songs

Tell the children that spiritual and gospel songs are religious (Christian) songs and were originally sung by African-Americans. Their history and purpose could be equated to the history and purpose of the folk song. Gospel choirs are very popular in Britain today. Play track 8 and ask them to join in clapping on the 'off' beat (marked with an X on the song sheet), which is played on the tambourine.

Learning the song

Teach both vocal lines of the song by rote using the recording. If you have a balance control you can isolate each part on the 'split vocals' track. You may notice that the singer on the recording does not always sing exactly the notes printed – especially in the lower of the two parts. This freedom to improvise around a melody is a strong characteristic of gospel singing and it does not matter if you sing the written part or the sung part.

Using the 'belt' voice

The singing on the recording is very powerful. If the children try to copy this timbre, they may have to use their 'shouting' or 'belt' voice. This 'good news' gospel song will take that type of singing because 'good news' should be shouted from the rooftops. However, if/when children use their belt voice it must be used cautiously and carefully as it can be very tiring to sing, and harsh and unmusical to listen to as they strain to reach the high notes. Try to ensure that the sound does not become so raucous that it prevents them from hearing themselves because this will result in singing out of tune. Encourage them to project their voices to the back of the room by breathing deeply and working harder with their abdominal muscles rather than forcing the sound.

Moving gospel style

As they sing, encourage the children to move freely to the pulse by swaying, finger clicking, moving from one foot to the other, etc. Lengthen the performance of the song by playing the backing track in the middle and at the end of the song, and ask some children to perform their scat singing. If there is an opportunity, invite a local gospel choir to give a concert in your school so that the children become more familiar with the style.

Achievement

Can sing in two parts. Can sing powerfully, not raucously. Can move, perform and present in the gospel style.

SONG SHEET 23

Good News

Traditional Spiritual

Good News (continued)

Good news, the char - iot's com-ing, And I don't want her leave - a me,

news, the char - iot's com-ing, And I don't want her leave - a me,

Don't want her leave - a me, Don't want her leave - a me be - hind.

Don't want her leave - a me, Don't want her leave - a me be - hind.

 Sounds of Singing Y5–6/P6–7 © Alison Ley, Nelson Thornes Ltd, 2004

Frame-works

This chapter looks at the importance of phrases. All music is thought of in phrases. A phrase in music is comparable to a phrase in language – it is a group of sounds that together make sense. The structure of a song helps to determine the overall arrangement and the dynamics, whilst the phrases help to determine the shape of the melody.

There is more work on diction – looking again at words to be sung at speed, needing clarity and agility, as well as using emphasis on words to be more expressive.

Movement is used to aid the memory for words and to help children to visualise and feel the structure of a song.

There is an opportunity to clap and to vocalise accompaniments in a Brazilian style, and a chance to sing in a foreign language and a British dialect.

There are three reasonably challenging part songs and two songs that require controlled unison singing.

Finally, children are introduced to a 'new' style of singing, namely crooning.

Lesson	Focus
Gossip	Incorporating visual and vocal expression with lyrics
	Conveying the humour of a song
	Articulating clearly and lightly
	Adding moves to aid the memory
	Singing a chromatic passage in tune
	Singing and holding a vocal part
Geordie's Penker and Jikel 'Emaweni	Listening with care to different speech sounds
	Singing in a regional accent
	Writing words phonetically
	Identifying and making click sounds
	Singing in a foreign language
Songs of the West (5)	Recognising and singing a chord sequence
	Singing in three parts
	Recognising and identifying structures
The White Cliffs of Dover	Learning about ballads
	Identifying phrases and breathing points
	Singing in a 'crooning' style
	Singing a solo
Song for Oxum	Identifying ostinato patterns
	Transferring instrumental sounds to vocal sounds
	Accompanying a song with vocal ostinato patterns
	Singing in another language

CHAPTER 4

Frameworks

Lesson 1

Gossip

Focus

Incorporating visual and vocal expression with lyrics. Conveying the humour of a song. Articulating clearly and lightly. Adding moves to aid the memory. Singing a chromatic passage in tune. Singing and holding a vocal part.

Resources

CD 2 tracks 10, 11, 12, 13; song sheets 25, 26.

About the song

A humorous song in the style of a 'patter' song.

Activities

Facial gymnastics

This song needs articulating with clarity, agility and lightness, so ask the children to loosen their facial muscles by inventing, and then doing, some tongue, eye, lip and facial exercises. (See 'All about warm-ups' on page xviii.)

Express your feelings

Display the lyrics from song sheet 26 on the board or projector. Say the words to the children, as if you were telling a gossipy humorous story. Put in as much dramatic feeling as you can possibly manage: 'ham' it up. Divide the class in two, and ask each half to say (all at the same time) alternate phrases to the other half giving their own, individual, 'over the top', expressive interpretation.

Chant it

Play track 11 several times and ask the children to mouth the words silently along with the recording, using exaggerated facial expressions to convey the humour of the song. They can also make up complementary movements for each phrase to help them remember the words. For example:

- 'Haven't you heard about?' – Put hand to ear.
- 'Didn't you read about?' – Put both hands side by side, palm upwards in front of body.
- 'Wasn't it sad about?' – Trace tear lines down cheeks.
- 'Ooh what a pain!' – Put hand on heart . . . etc.

When the words and rhythms are memorised, the children can chant out loud. Ask them to articulate every word lightly, working the lips, tongue and teeth overtime.

Singing expressively

Sing the song in unison maintaining the light, clear articulation and facial expressions. If the children are having problems in singing section D in tune, play the Gossip warm-ups (tracks 12 and 13) and asking them to copy the exercises.

Divide the class into three groups and sing Gossip in parts structured like the recording:

- All groups sing all the sections through once.
- Group C sing/say their part all the way through fading at the end.
- Group A sing their part three more times.
- Group B sing coming in after group A has sung their part just once.

A→B→C→D (everyone) →C→C+A together→C+A+B together→C+A together→C repeating and fading away.

Achievement

Can put visual and vocal expression into lyrics. Can convey humour through music. Can articulate with clarity. Can incorporate movement into a song. Can sing a chromatic passage in tune. Can hold a part.

SONG SHEET 25

Gossip

Words and music by Nick Curtis

SONG SHEET 26

Gossip (continued)

Haven't you heard about,
Didn't you read about,
Wasn't it sad about,
Ooh what a pain!
Never tell them about,
What do you think about,
Guess what she said about,
Never again!

Don't tell her I told you so!
He said, 'Really, yes I know!'
Well I never! Ooh my word!
That's outrageous! So I've heard.

Gossip away, gossip away, gossip and gossip and gossip away!
Gossip away, gossip away, gossip and gossip and gossip away!

Tell us some more, heard it before, here we go again!

50

Geordie's Penker and Jikel 'Emaweni

Focus

Listening with care to different speech sounds. Singing in a regional accent. Writing words phonetically. Identifying and making click sounds. Singing in a foreign language.

Resources

CD 2 tracks 14, 15, 16, 17; song sheets 27, 28, 29.

About the song

Geordie's Penker

This humorous folk song is sung in a regional accent and uses dialect words. A 'penker' is a marble, 'double row' is a double terrace of houses, and a 'cundy' is a drainpipe (conduit).

Jikel 'Emaweni

This is a work song from South Africa. It would be sung to accompany the rhythmic movements of a group employed in building, digging, quarrying and so on.

Activities

Copying a regional accent

Play Geordie's Penker (track 14) and ask the children to listen very carefully to the pronunciation of the words, in particular the last line of each verse. Now ask them to say the last line, copying the accent exactly. Play the song again and let them join in, singing the last line and still mimicking the accent.

Aids to pronunciation

Many folk and traditional songs are passed down from generation to generation through the aural tradition. Sometimes the exact pronunciation of the words is written down phonetically.

Arrange the children into small groups and appoint a scribe to each group. Play Nonsense Words (track 15) and ask them to listen very carefully to the pronunciation of each word. Pause after each word so that each group can discuss how they will write it phonetically. Discuss various phonetic versions of the same word, including the following examples: dopolop, teckizing, klacack, mowa, yickoo, splishow, flarelala, brrrk. Decide which spelling works the best and why. Do not worry about the phonetic realisation conforming to 'standard' phonetics; as long as the children can understand their own representation, that is all that is required. Now listen again to Geordie's Penker and ask them to write down the last line in phonetics.

Singing in a foreign language

It is often easier for a group to sing in a foreign language than in their own, as everyone can learn to pronounce the words in exactly the same way with no individual accents to eliminate. Play Jikel 'Emaweni (track 16) several times to familiarise the children with the melody and ask them to identify exactly where the clicks come in the words of the song (see song sheet 28). Play track 17, pausing after each line to allow the children to copy exactly and to memorise the words they hear on the recording. Once the children know the words write the phonetic lyrics on the board (written under the lyrics) so that they can relate the written word to the aural sound.

Achievement

Can listen accurately to different speech sounds. Can copy a regional accent. Can write vocal sounds phonetically. Can identify click sounds. Can sing foreign words with accuracy.

SONG SHEET 27

Geordie's Penker

Folk song from Tyneside

Wor   Geor - die's   lost   his   pen - ker,

Wor   Geor - die's   lost   his   pen - ker,

Wor   Geor - die's   lost   his   pen - ker,

Doon   the   dou - ble   row.

2. It's rolled reet down the cundy (x3)
Doon the double row.

3. I reached but couldn't get it (x3)
Doon the double row.

4. So I went and got a clothes-prop (x3)
Doon the double row.

5. And I rammed it the cundy (x3)
Doon the double row.

6. But still it wouldn't fetch it (x3)
Doon the double row.

7. So I went and got gunpowder (x3)
Doon the double row.

8. And I rammed it up the cundy (x3)
Doon the double row.

9. And I set light to the powder (x3)
Doon the double row.

10. There's nowt left of the cundy (x3)
Doon the double row.

11. Wor Geordie's found his penker (x3)
Doon the double row.

12. It's in his trousers pocket (x3)
Doon the double row.

Jikel 'Emaweni

Folk song from South Africa

English translation:

Throw it into the slope, I am leaving.
Throw it into the slope, I am leaving.
The men threw, threw it into the slope,
They threw it to Radebe, they threw it into the slope.

SONG SHEET 29

Exotic Language Sounds

In some languages that are spoken in South Africa, most notably Xhosa (Nelson Mandela's native language) and Zulu, the speech is sprinkled with exotic and unusual sounds that we do not ordinarily think of as speech sounds. A collection of clicking, popping, clucking and smacking sounds, generically known as 'clicks', are sounded along with the expected vowels and consonants. Nearly all speech sounds in languages around the world are an interruption of the air stream coming from the lungs. With the 'clicks' the air stream is not coming out, but for a split second it is being sucked in.

There are three basic clicks in the Xhosa language, shown by the letters 'x', 'q' and 'c', and another fifteen variations! Those who are not able to master the 'x' click in 'Xhosa' pronounce it as 'caw-suh' or 'haw-suh'.

Ask the children to try making the three basic clicks.

1. The 'x' click is a 'side click' produced by placing the tip of the tongue against the front part of the roof of the mouth, then pulling the tongue downwards and outwards, allowing air to escape on both sides of the tongue – similar to the sound you make when you are trying to get a horse to go faster.
2. The 'q' click is a 'top click' produced by placing the tongue in the middle of the roof of the mouth, then pulling the tongue down quickly while keeping the mouth in an open 'O' shape – a bit like the sound of a cork popping.
3. The 'c' click is a 'front click' produced by placing the tip of the tongue behind the upper front teeth and then pulling the tongue downward while forming the lips into a slightly parted smile – it sounds similar to the sound you make when you express pity.

None of these sounds is very loud, so do not try too hard and you should get the right effect!

Frameworks

Songs of the West (5)

Focus

Recognising and singing a chord sequence. Singing in three parts. Recognising and identifying structures.

Resources

CD 1 tracks 21, 22, 11, 12, 13; song sheets 10, 11 (pages 19–20).

About the song

Three traditional American folk songs. See Chapter 1 lesson 5.

Activities

Singing a three-note chord

To prepare the children for singing in three parts, listen to track 21. The singer sings three different sets of notes four times each and then combines all three sets. Divide the class into three groups and allocate one set of notes to each group.

- The first group sings the first phrase (G G G F# G).
- The second group sings the second phrase (B C¹ B A B).
- The third group sings the third phrase (D¹ E¹ D¹ D¹ D¹).

Ask each group to sing their part, to 'noo', with the singer on the recording. When the children are confident, sing all three simultaneously.

Three or more notes sung together are known as a chord. The above chords are sung in the same order in Midnight Special, though not with the same frequency. A succession of chords is known as a 'chord sequence' (see glossary). Repeat the chord sequence over and over so that they can feel the richness of the sound they are making.

Learning the third part

Use track 22 to help the children learn the third harmony part (counter-melody) of Midnight Special. When rehearsing, it could be helpful to sing this to 'la', unaccompanied and at a much slower speed. When the children feel confident, sing it up to speed with the recording.

When all three Midnight Special parts are secure, try singing two parts together in any and all combinations, finally singing all three parts together.

Moving to structures

In Rock Island Line, ask the children to invent two simple, contrasting hand movements to show the difference between the verse and the refrain.

In Midnight Special, the 1st phrase 'A' is answered by the 2nd phrase 'B'. These phrases are heard first in unison, then in two parts and finally in three parts. Ask the children to suggest some simple movement to reflect this structure.

In Worried Man, help the children to decide which two melodic phrases of the verse and the refrain are exactly the same (*the first and the third*). Ask them to give each of the four phrases a letter name. (*ABAC. Repeated phrases should have the same letter.*) There are three verses. Invite the children to suggest some simple movements to reflect this structure.

Play the Songs of the West all the way through for the children to perform their movements.

Achievement

Can recognise a chord sequence. Can sing in three parts. Can understand and recognise the structure of a song.

CHAPTER 4

Frameworks

Lesson 4

The White Cliffs of Dover

Focus

Learning about ballads. Identifying phrases and breathing points. Singing in a 'crooning' style. Singing a solo.

Resources

CD 2 tracks 18, 19; song sheets 30, 31, 32.

About the song

A very popular ballad in World War Two, made famous by Dame Vera Lynn.

Activities

About ballads

Play the recording of The White Cliffs of Dover (track 18) and discuss its origins and lyrics. Explain to the children that a ballad is a sentimental song. There is only one verse, and that usually sets the scene and explains the story. Very few people ever remember the words of the verse, but the refrain, which gives the mood and feeling, is the part that is always remembered. Thank You For the Music (Chapter 6) is another song with the same structure.

Finding the phrases and breathing points

Arrange the children in groups of three or four. Make a copy of the song lyrics available to each group. Play the song two or three more times and, as they listen, ask the children to mark on the sheet where they think the phrases should begin and end, and where they think they should breathe. (For your information, the phrase marks and breathing points are shown on song sheets 30 and 31.) The breathing on the recording occurs in the middle of phrases as well as at the end, even though the words in some of the phrases imply that there should be no break in the melodic line, e.g. 'And Jimmy will go to sleep in his own little bed again'. This very relaxed style of singing, which is known as 'crooning', allows the singer the latitude to interpret the song in a more casual manner. However, the breathing is not so dominant that it interrupts the melodic line or the continuity of the phrases. When singing this song, if the children want to breathe through a phrase rather than in the middle of it, that is also quite correct.

Triplets

Play the 'new' version of the song on track 19 and then the original version again (track 18). Listen carefully to the difference between the two. When crooning, it is important to sing the rhythm like the original, more relaxed, version (a triplet) and not in the more regimented style of the 'new' one (crotchet followed by two quavers).

Singing with feeling

Play the original version of the song and ask the children to stand up, adopt a good singing position and join in with the refrain, being careful to breathe in the agreed places. Remember to emphasise the feeling of sentimentality and hopefulness in the song, but do not make it too soppy. When crooning, the words still have to be really well articulated with short consonants, long unified vowels, and long sounds on the first vowel of any diphthong. Some children may like to sing the verse as a solo.

Achievement

Can understand the structure of a typical 'ballad'. Can identify phrases and breathing points. Can sing in a crooning style. Can sing a solo.

The White Cliffs of Dover

Words by Nat Burton
Music by Walter Kent

SONG SHEET 31

The White Cliffs of Dover (continued)

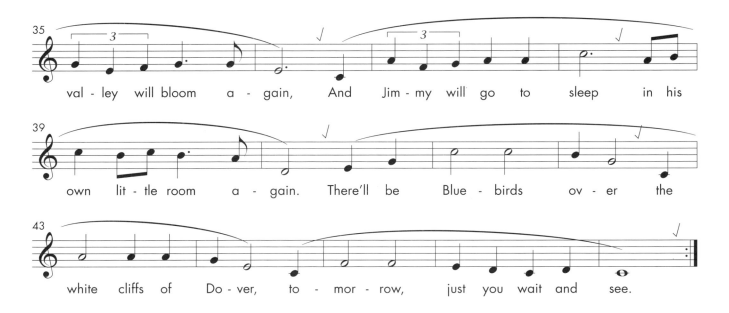

val - ley will bloom a - gain, And Jim - my will go to sleep in his

own lit - tle room a - gain. There'll be Blue - birds ov - er the

white cliffs of Do - ver, to - mor - row, just you wait and see.

The White Cliffs of Dover (continued)

I'll never forget the people I met braving those angry skies;

I remember well as the shadows fell, the light of hope in their eyes.

And tho' I'm far away, I still can hear them say, 'Thumbs up!'

For when the dawn comes up:

There'll be Bluebirds over the white cliffs of Dover,

Tomorrow, just you wait and see.

There'll be love and laughter and peace ever after,

Tomorrow, when the world is free.

The shepherd will tend his sheep, the valley will bloom again,

And Jimmy will go to sleep in his own little room again.

There'll be Bluebirds over the white cliffs of Dover,

Tomorrow, just you wait and see.

CHAPTER 4

Frameworks

Lesson 5

Song for Oxum

Focus

Identifying ostinato patterns. Transferring instrumental sounds to vocal sounds. Accompanying a song with vocal ostinato patterns. Singing in another language.

Resources

CD 2 tracks 20, 21; song sheet 33.

About the song

A traditional song from Brazil. 'Oxum' is pronounced 'Oh-shoom'. This song is performed during the carnivals held in Brazil every February. The song is for a beautiful African goddess of the waters, still worshipped by the descendants of the Nigerian slaves who were taken to Brazil hundreds of years ago. The words were taken down phonetically from a Brazilian folk singer. The language is unknown.

Activities

Background to the song

Listen to the song (track 20) and discuss the background. Practise saying the lyrics.

Clapping rhythms

Ask the children to time the very long introduction, the instrumental break in the middle and the long ending. Do the same again, so they can double-check their answers (*55 seconds, 10 seconds and 46 seconds, respectively*). Ask them what instruments are playing (*high-and-low pitched conga drums; cabassa; two-tone metal agogo*). Now listen to all three rhythm patterns being played one after the other, on track 21, and help the children to learn them by heart. The third rhythm is especially tricky; don't worry if some children are unable to do this with complete accuracy. Now play the song again and ask them to identify the instruments (*1st rhythm = conga drums; 2nd rhythm = cabassa; 3rd rhythm = metal agogo*).

Vocalising rhythms

Divide the class into three groups and ask each group to make a vocal sound to imitate one of the instruments (e.g. 'bom ba ba' for the drum; 'tsh cht cht' for the cabassa; 'tick-tock' for the metal agogo). Chant the ostinato (repeated) rhythms, separately at first, and when secure, put all three together.

Singing with a vocal backing

Help the children to learn the song, taking care to keep the rhythms tight in bars 5 and 7 and listening carefully for the pronunciation of the words. Give half the class the vocal chant to perform as an accompaniment, and let the other half sing the song. Keep the accompaniment light and rhythmically steady. It may help to tap some claves on the steady beat to keep everyone together.

Achievement

Can identify ostinato patterns. Can transfer instrumental sounds to vocal sounds. Can chant an ostinato accompaniment to a song. Can sing in a foreign language.

Song for Oxum

Traditional song from Brazil

ABOUT CHAPTER 5

Go with the flow

This chapter focuses on understanding pitch. It looks at the relationship between pitch, mood and lyrics and the way they influence the musical interpretation (the expression) of a song.

It covers note clashes or scrunches (suspensions) and their role in building up tension and excitement, and it looks at the peaceful effect that singing in thirds (three notes apart) has on the mood of a song. The technique required to sing high notes is revised, as is the skill of staggered breathing.

There are songs to illustrate the way pitch is used to determine the overall structure of a song, how it is used in imitation and how it is used to emphasise important words in the lyrics. There is more work on the art of shaping each phrase, like waves rising and falling.

Children's aural skills, and their understanding of chords, are developed with a two-chord sequence, which is used as a basis for vocal improvisation.

Four songs are sung in parts, and there is an excellent five-part song (not difficult!) that has been especially written to address the challenge of reading notation.

Lesson	Focus
Evening Prayer	Learning about the structure and musical features
	Understanding the relationship between pitch and interpretation (expression)
	Shaping phrases
	Singing a two-part song
Matilda	Clapping the calypso rhythm
	Recognising chords
	Vocal improvisation over two chords
	Singing a solo
Notin' Around	Understanding about the basic note values
	Understanding time signatures
	Staggering the breathing
	Singing in five parts
Songs of the West (6)	Opening the mouth 'north–south'
	Learning how to sing high notes
	Singing in two parts
Turn, Turn, Turn	Understanding the relationship between pitch, mood and lyrics
	Singing in canon

62

Go with the flow

Evening Prayer

Focus

Learning about the structure and musical features. Understanding the relationship between pitch and interpretation (expression). Shaping phrases. Singing a two-part song.

Resources

CD 2 tracks 22, 23, 24, 25; song sheets 34, 35.

About the song

This duet comes from the opera *Hansel and Gretel* by the German composer Engelbert Humperdinck (1854–1921). This song is sung when Hansel and Gretel are forced to sleep in the woods. They are tired, frightened and lost.

Activities

Play track 22 and discuss the story of Hansel and Gretel. Talk about the lyrics and mood of the song and where it fits into the story.

Recognising four different musical features

Play the song several times. You may like to hand out or project the song sheet so that you can identify and talk about the following musical features.

The song is in two halves. In the first section (bars 1–8, up to 'guiding') the two voices are almost running parallel and most of the time they are just three notes apart. This gives a solid and comforting feel.

In bars 9–21 the second voice roughly echoes or 'imitates' the first voice but at a lower pitch. We are kept on the edge of our seat anticipating that the second voice will catch up with the first voice, which it eventually does at the very last note.

Play track 24 and ask the children to listen for all the note clashes or 'scrunches' that occur. They are marked with a star on the song sheet. When notes clash in this way they sound good because you anticipate them moving on (resolving) to the very next harmonious non-clashing pair of notes. This tension and resolution is musically exciting and very satisfying.

Point out that the melody for this song reflects the lyrics. The beginning of the song is quiet and low in pitch as Hansel and Gretel sing about two angels guarding them; the volume increases and the pitch rises as they sing about each additional pair of angels, reaching the climax of the whole song on the word 'Heaven' in the penultimate bar. 'You'll Never Walk Alone' (chapter 1 lessons 3 and 4) is another song that does this.

Singing with feeling

For rehearsal purposes, vocal tracks only are played on track 24, and the separate parts are played on instruments on track 25. If you have a balance control you can use it with track 23 to isolate the individual vocal parts. Remind the children to:

- breathe at the end of phrases;
- give each phrase a musical shape, as in the warm-up exercise;
- make the climax strong, but not over-loud and ugly;
- be careful not to run words into each other, especially if the second word begins with a vowel;
- sing each part well in unison before attempting to put the parts together;
- be careful to keep the pitch up in bars 18 to 20.

Achievement

Can understand about the structure and musical features. Can understand the relationship between interpretation and pitch. Can sing with expression. Can hold a second part.

SONG SHEET 34

Evening Prayer

Engelbert Humperdinck
Words translated by C. Bache

1. When at night I go to sleep, Four-teen an-gels watch do keep,
2. When at night I go to sleep, Four-teen an-gels watch do keep,

2. Two my head are guard-ing, Two my feet are guid-ing,
   Two my head are guard-ing, Two my feet are guid-ing,

3. Two are on my right hand, Two are on my left hand,
   Two are on my right hand, Two are on my

4. Two who warm-ly co-ver, Two who o'er me hov-er,
   left hand Two who warm-ly cov-er, Two who o'er me

Evening Prayer (continued)

CHAPTER 5

Go with the flow

Lesson 2

Matilda

Focus

Clapping the calypso rhythm. Recognising chords. Vocal improvisation over two chords. Singing a solo.

Resources

CD 2 tracks 26, 27, 28; song sheet 36.

About the song

A traditional Jamaican folk song.

Activities

Calypso clap

Play 'Matilda' (track 26) and listen to the calypso rhythm. The word 'Matilda' is sung in calypso rhythm every time it occurs. Play the song at least four more times, and ask the children to clap the calypso rhythm on each 'Matilda'. At first it may seem difficult, but it will soon become second nature to do this.

Identifying chords

Encourage the children to join in with the refrain. Explain that each time they sing the word 'Matilda', they are singing the separated notes of a chord. The first time it is the chord of C, the second time the chord of F and the third, the chord of G. A chord is a simultaneous combination of notes, usually at least three.

Improvising over chord patterns

When a chord is played it is not difficult to make up tunes to go with the chord. Play track 27 to the children. The singer is making up her own tune to go with the different chords, and then, after 16 bars, she fades away as the instruments fade away. Encourage the children to make up and to hum their own tunes as track 28 (instruments only – no vocal) is played. Play this over and over again, and repeat the exercise frequently until the children gain some confidence in being able to feel and to find the right notes to go with the chords. This can only be achieved when the wrong notes, as well as the right notes, can be heard, and this requires regular practice. You may like to use an electric keyboard to play a one-note chord accompaniment and ask the children to improvise sung phrases as you play. Try using one, two or all three of the following chords: D minor (notes D F A), C major (notes C E G), and E minor (notes E G B). Do not, however use just C and E minor; that is not a very musical or sympathetic combination.

Solos

Ask for individual or small groups of children to sing the verses, paying special attention to the West Indian accent. Ask for other volunteers to use maracas or another shaker to play the calypso rhythm all the way through the song. Ask the rest of the class to sing the refrain.

Achievement

Can clap a calypso rhythm. Can recognise and understand the composition of a chord. Can improvise over a two chord sequence. Can sing a solo.

Matilda

2. My money was to buy me house and land,
   The woman she got a serious plan.
   Matilda, she take me money and run Venezuela.

3. Now the money was safe in me bed,
   Stuck in the pillow beneath me head,
   But Matilda, she find me money and run Venezuela.

4. Never will I love again,
   All me money gone in vain
   'Cos Matilda, she take me money and run Venezuela.

CHAPTER 5

Go with the flow

Lesson 3

Notin' Around

Focus

Understanding about the basic note values. Understanding time signatures. Staggering the breathing. Singing in five parts.

Resources

CD 2 tracks 29, 30; song sheets 37, 38; information sheet 2.

About the song

A specially written children's song and great for learning basic note values.

Activities

Reading the notation

Play track 29. Hand out or project the song sheets and ask the children to follow the words and melody of Notin' Around. This is a great song for learning basic note values. In nearly all countries except the UK, notes are called whole, half, quarter, eighth and sixteenth notes, which makes it much easier to learn and remember the values. The information sheet explains the note names and values. Remind the children that the top number of the time signature at the start of a song gives the number of beats (or counts or claps that should be made before the children start singing) in a bar, and the bottom figure tells us if the claps are half notes (2) quarter notes (4) or eighth notes (8).

Staggered breathing

After listening to the song recording a few times, help the whole class to practise Section 4 on its own. They will all need to breathe in different places, i.e. stagger their breathing. They should get quieter before they run out of breath; when they begin to sing again, they should do so quietly and slowly gradually getting louder until they are singing at the same volume as the rest of the class. Help the children to learn Section 4 as follows:

- Chant the words in the word rhythms of the song; do this until the words are articulated rhythmically and with precision and can be said from memory.
- Sing the melody slowly and unaccompanied, to 'la'.
- Combine the words and melody, still singing slowly.
- Sing the section up to speed and stagger the breathing.

Most children will want to breathe after two bars, which will create a drop in volume. To avoid this, ask some children to breathe at the end of the first bar.

Learning the rest of the song

Explain that, to begin with, everybody will learn all five sections and sing them in unison. Teach the children a section at a time. Breathe in the places marked on the song sheet. To sing the song in parts, divide the class into five groups with each group being allocated one section. Put any two parts together (e.g. sections 2 and 3, or sections 4 and 2, or sections 1 and 5, etc.), then any three sections together. Finally have all five sections singing together. The structure of the song on the recording is:

- Everyone sings all five sections in unison
- Section 1 sings their part × 5.
- Section 2 sings their part × 4.
- Section 3 sings their part × 3.
- Section 4 sings their part × 2.
- Section 5 sings their part × 1.

As each section enters, they should sing with strength and projection (sing to the back of the room and use plenty of abdominal muscles to support the air) but drop the volume on their repeated entries.

Achievement

Can understand and recognise the value of notes. Can understand time signatures. Can stagger their breathing. Can hold down one of five parts.

Notin' Around

Words and music by Shena Power

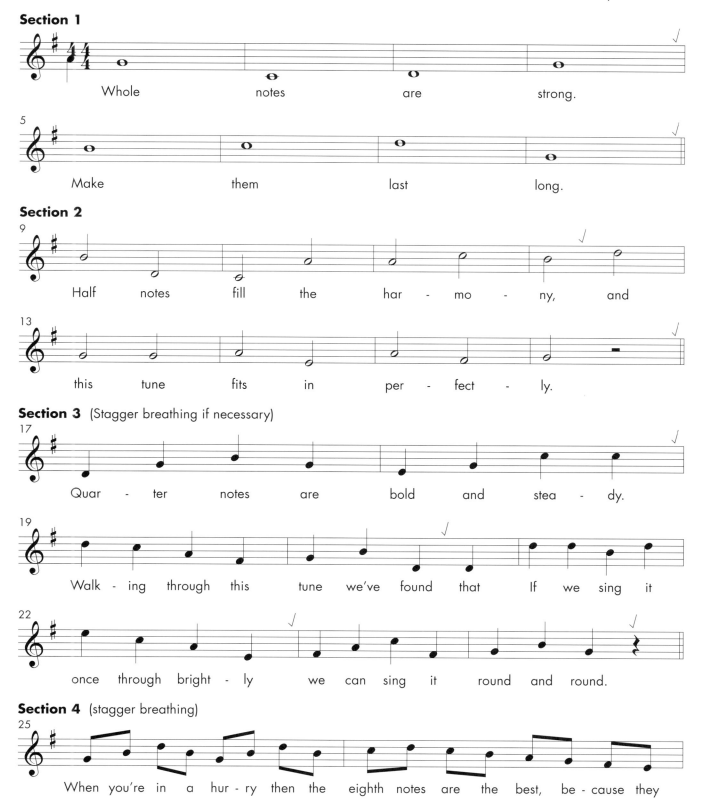

Section 1

Whole notes are strong.

Make them last long.

Section 2

Half notes fill the har - mo - ny, and

this tune fits in per - fect - ly.

Section 3 (Stagger breathing if necessary)

Quar - ter notes are bold and stea - dy.

Walk - ing through this tune we've found that If we sing it

once through bright - ly we can sing it round and round.

Section 4 (stagger breathing)

When you're in a hur - ry then the eighth notes are the best, be - cause they

SONG SHEET 38

Notin' Around (continued)

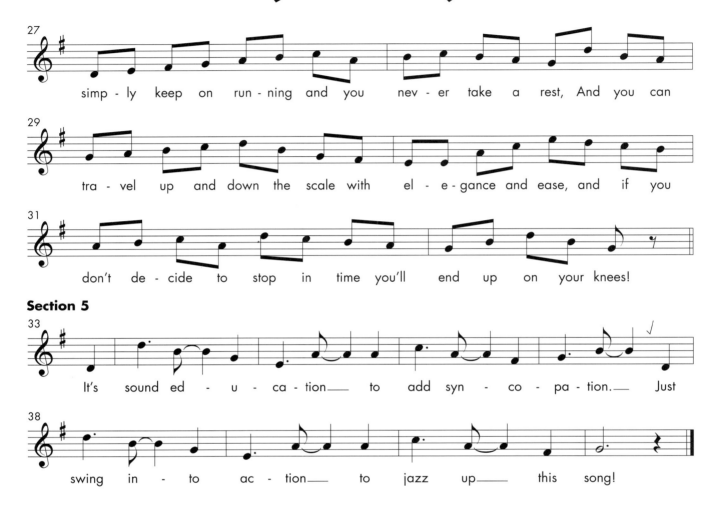

Section 5

Sounds of Singing Y5–6/P6–7 © Alison Ley, Nelson Thornes Ltd, 2004

INFORMATION SHEET 2

Note names

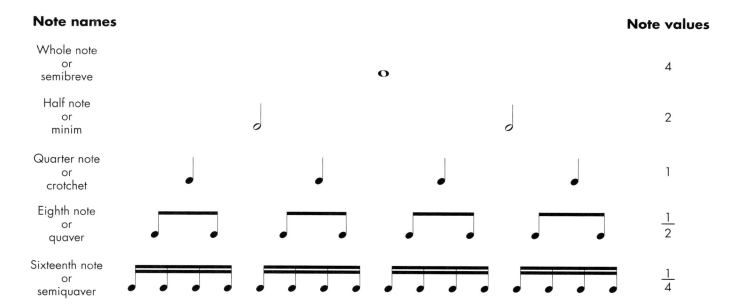

Note names	Note values
Whole note or semibreve	4
Half note or minim	2
Quarter note or crotchet	1
Eighth note or quaver	$\frac{1}{2}$
Sixteenth note or semiquaver	$\frac{1}{4}$

CHAPTER 5

Go with the flow

Lesson 4

Songs of the West (6)

Focus

Opening the mouth 'north–south'. Learning how to sing high notes. Singing in two parts.

Resources

CD 1 tracks 23, 24, 14; song sheets 12, 13 (pages 21–2).

About the song

Three traditional American folk songs. See Chapter 1 lesson 5.

Activities

North–south mouths

Do some general face and mouth warm-ups (see All about warm-ups, page xviii).

Ask the children to yawn and to feel the cold air go down their throat. Now ask them to face a partner and to say 'bah ——', i.e. holding the 'ah' sound on for a slow count of four. Their mouths should be comfortably wide open, from north–south and not east–west – in fact exactly as if they were yawning. Let them check each other to see that they have the right open mouth shape and are not pointing their heads up in the air. With a stick (a paintbrush, beater or ruler) draw the flight of a fly whizzing around the room. Ask the children to imagine that they have a laser beam coming from their open throat and the laser beam has to follow the path of the fly. When the fly flies, they sing 'bah', matching the pitch of their voices to reflect the highs and lows of the fly's path. (Do not point too high or the children will point their head upwards.) Every time the fly settles they have to try and zap it with the laser beam, to a short 'bah' sound.

Preparing for high notes

To sing higher notes you need to stand with the right posture, take enough breath, have a nice open mouth and be ready to give a little extra support (push) with the abdomen muscles (see Chapter 1 lessons 3 and 4). Ask the children to listen and then to copy the High Notes warm-up activity (track 23). They should sing to 'loo', crescendo (get louder) going up to the top note and diminuendo (get quieter) coming down. Not all children will reach the high notes; this is normal but, as with all physical activities, the more they practise the more success they will have.

Learning the second part

Play the second and third verses of Worried Man and ask the children to listen to the second part. (If you have a balance control you can use it with track 24 to separate the vocal parts.) When they feel ready, ask them to quietly hum the part with the recording. Once the part is well known sing it to the words. Remind the children that to reach the high notes they should work their abdominal muscles a little harder.

Putting it all together

When the children are confident, see if they can sing both parts with the recording. The higher notes need not be sung loudly – they should complement the main tune, not overpower it. Eventually, use track 14 with the balance control to remove the vocals and play the accompaniment only to support a sung performance of The Songs of the West.

Achievement

Can sing with a north–south open mouth. Can understand how to sing high notes. Can sing high notes. Can sing a second harmony part.

Go with the flow

Turn, Turn, Turn

Focus

Understanding the relationship between pitch, mood and lyrics. Singing in canon.

Resources

CD 2 tracks 31, 32, 33; song sheet 39.

About the song

This song was composed in 1954 by Pete Seeger. The words are adapted from the Bible (The Book of Ecclesiastes Chapter 3). A great social campaigner, he cultivated a folk music revival in the 1950s, composing such songs as 'If I had a Hammer', and 'Where Have all the Flowers Gone?' His variation of an old spiritual, which he called 'We Shall Overcome', has become an anthem of the crusade for equality in America.

Activities

Learning the refrain

To warm up the children's voices, ask them to sing up and down an eight-note scale (e.g. C to C[1] and back). Half the class sings the first note of the scale and holds it as a drone while the other half sings slowly up the scale to the sound 'oo'. Ask the children to listen to the effect. Swap over. (There is an example of this on track 31.)

Play track 32 to the children and talk about the meaning of the lyrics. Ask them to join in with the refrain as soon as they are able. Practise the very first entry and make sure that they all come in together after the introduction.

Watch out for the following singing traps:

* Breathe only in the marked places.
* Do not breathe after the word 'purpose'.
* Sing through the word 'turn' each time it appears.
* Give each phrase a musical shape increasing the dynamics to the highest note and fading slightly at the end of the phrase.
* Hold on to the 'i' sound of 'every*thing*' for as long as possible, before closing on the 'ng' sound.
* Keep the singing lively even though the pitch is quite low.
* Do not allow the children to use their shouting (belt) voice.

Relating pitch to mood and lyrics

Discuss with the children why the refrain has a low, downward flowing melody, and the verses have a melody that stays high pitched throughout. (*The 'low impact' refrain reiterates a philosophical thought, which is the main focus of the song. The verses elaborate on this thought, raising the pitch to excite the listener to agree and to be inspired – just as we raise the pitch of our voices in speech when we are excited about something. The incessant repetition of the note C has the same effect as when somebody constantly repeats something they are saying in order to make sure that the listener really understands.*) Talk about the effectiveness of this use of pitch as a way of enhancing the lyrics.

Canonic entry

Ask the children to sing the verses as soon as they feel confident enough to do so. In the second verse, the second melody starts after the first and imitates it exactly. This exact imitation is known as singing in 'canon' (see also Chapter 3 lesson 4). Encourage a 'smiley' face (see All about singing, page xiii), good posture and deep/low breathing to avoid singing flat on the repeated Cs and on the last phrase which goes down a scale. Every time the word 'A' occurs, make sure it is separated from the previous word – i.e. that the two words do not run into each other.

Achievement

Can understand the relationship between pitch, mood and lyrics. Can sing in canon.

SONG SHEET 39

Turn, Turn, Turn

Words from the Book of Ecclesiastes
Adaptation and music by Pete Seeger

Sounds of Singing Y5–6/P6–7 © Alison Ley, Nelson Thornes Ltd, 2004

ABOUT CHAPTER 6

Sing what you mean

This chapter explores how a composer creates the mood and character of a song, and it challenges the children to decide how to interpret a song. It stresses the importance of thinking and singing in phrases, and asks the children to identify the correct breathing points in a couple of songs. It also looks at the value of giving phrases a musical shape.

Opportunities are provided to sing and perform given dynamics in a more sophisticated and musical manner.

It shows how the use of low and high pitches will affect the mood of a song, and how repeated pitches can give a sense of anticipation.

Lyrics are spoken, as if telling an interesting or exciting story. When the lyrics are subsequently sung, they retain that drama and excitement adding more to the expressive quality of the song.

There are exercises for achieving unified vowels, exercises in perfecting difficult rhythms, dance routines, two-part songs and a challenging way of singing a round.

There are two Christmas songs in this chapter. Now Light One Thousand Christmas Lights contains Christian religious references while Christmas is Coming is secular in nature. Vesper Hymn comes from the Russian Christian tradition and, depending on the children in your class, you may wish to amend some of the lyrics.

Lesson	Focus
Vesper Hymn	Identifying the breathing points
	Singing a musically shaped phrase
	Observing the dynamics
	Singing unanimous vowels and clear consonants
	Singing a legato descant
Christmas is Coming	Saying and singing words with expression
	Singing rhythmically and in a slightly detached style
	Using consonants to help projection
	Singing a round
	Singing a round whilst walking round the room
Now Light One Thousand Christmas Lights	Deciding on dynamics Listening for, and performing with, a good blend and tonal quality
	Extending the song
Songs of the West (7)	Identifying important words
	Recognising how musical features change the mood and add variety to a song

Lesson	Focus
	Deciding the best dynamics and expressive features
	Singing a solo or singing in a small group
Thank You For the Music	Understanding how a composer uses musical features to create the desired effect
	Following the contour of a melody
	Creating a dance routine
	Presenting and performing
We're Going to the Country	Identifying the character and expression of the song
	Clapping the word rhythms
	Accurately pitching notes
	Singing with a different accent
	Singing in two parts
	Dramatising the story

Sing what you mean

Vesper Hymn

Focus

Identifying the breathing points. Singing a musically shaped phrase. Observing the dynamics. Singing unanimous vowels and clear consonants. Singing a legato descant.

Resources

CD 3 tracks 1, 2, 3; song sheets 40, 41.

About the song

This is an old European tune. 'Vesper' is Latin for 'evening', and 'Vespers' is the sixth of seven church services during the day. The vesper bell was rung to call people to prayer.

Activities

The breathing points

Play Vesper Hymn (track 1) to the children and ask them to listen for breathing places. Play it again, using the pause button after each line, and ask the children to identify the breathing places. (*The places are marked on the song sheet.*) Play the hymn again, and ask the children to raise their hand each time a breath is taken. Now ask the children to hum the melody making sure they breathe in the right places (see Chapter 1 lesson 1 for information about correct humming technique).

The rocking melody

Ask the children to sing the words with the recording. This melody has bell-like patterns and a gentle rocking feel to it. In the first two lines, it constantly returns to the note B♭, i.e. on the syllables 'the, 'per', 'is', 'ing', 'the', 'ters', etc. These syllables are not important, but the syllables before each B♭, 'Hark', 'ves', 'hymn', 'steal', 'O'er', etc. are the important ones. This gentle rocking feel is maintained throughout the song, so the children should be careful not to accent or weight the non-important syllables and notes.

The dynamics

Listen again to the song, and ask the children to describe the dynamics. (*The hymn starts quietly, and gradually gets louder until the end of the third line. The fourth line is quiet and slightly mysterious, but the last line starts loud with a diminuendo (getting quieter) at the end.*)

The words

The beauty of this hymn will be spoilt if the vowels are not as pure and unanimous as possible. Use the song sheet or write the words of the first verse on the board and ask the children to underline or highlight the vowels. Listen to the Vesper warm-up (track 2). The singer is singing the words without any consonants. Play just one line and ask the children to copy the singer exactly. They will have to listen very carefully and should only move on to the next line when they understand what they are trying to accomplish. Watch out for all the words that begin with a vowel and clearly separate them from the previous word. Practise this frequently, and with any other song to improve the vowels, the blend and the tonal quality.

The descant

Listen to the descant being sung on track 3. The high notes will require the children to adopt a good singing posture. They must also remember to take the right amount of breath for each phrase and think of the high notes in their head before they sing them. Teach the descant line by line, singing it very smoothly (legato) to 'ah', and reminding the children to maintain the same dynamics as above. Choose a few children (or ask for volunteers) to sing the descant while the rest of the class sings the main tune.

Achievement

Can identify the breathing points. Can sing with expression. Can observe dynamics. Can understand about vowels with no consonants, unanimous vowels, and clear consonants. Can sing a descant.

SONG SHEET 40

Vesper Hymn

Old European tune
Words by Thomas Moore

1. Hark, the ves - per hymn is steal - ing O'er the wa - ters soft and clear;

Near - er yet and near - er peal - ing, Soft it breaks up - on the ear.

Sing ho - san - nah, Sing ho - san - nah, Sing ho - san - nah, A - men!

Far - ther now, now far - ther steal - ing, Soft it fades up - on the ear.

Sing ho - san - nah, Sing ho - san - nah, Sing ho - san - nah, A - men!

2. Now like moonlight, waves retreating To the shore it dies along;

    Now like angry surges meeting Breaks the mingled tide of song.

    Sing hosannah, sing hosannah, Sing hosannah, amen!

    Hark! Again like waves retreating To the shore, it dies along.

    Sing hosannah, sing hosannah, Sing hosannah, amen!

   Sounds of Singing Y5–6/P6–7 © Alison Ley, Nelson Thornes Ltd, 2004

Vesper Hymn Descant

(1. Hark, the ves-per hymn is steal-ing O'er the wa-ters soft and clear;

Near-er yet and near-er peal-ing, Soft it breaks up - on the ear.

Sing ho-san-nah, Sing ho-san-nah, Sing ho-san-nah, A - men!

Far - ther now, now far - ther steal-ing, Soft it fades up - on the ear.

Sing ho-san-nah, Sing ho-san-nah, Sing ho-san-nah, A - men!)

CHAPTER 6

Sing what you mean

Lesson 2

Christmas is Coming

Focus

Saying and singing words with expression. Singing rhythmically and in a slightly detached style. Using consonants to help projection. Singing a round. Singing a round whilst walking round the room.

Resources

CD 3 tracks 4, 5, 6; song sheet 42; one cymbal (optional).

About the song

A traditional Christmas round.

Activities

Learning the words

Play the first 33 seconds of track 4 (up to the second 'God bless you'), then stop the recording and repeat that same section of the song several more times until the children can sing the song in unison (i.e. not as a round) and they know the words from memory.

Breaking good news

When the words are secure, play track 6 and ask the children to listen to the words of the song being spoken with enthusiasm and expression. Now ask the children to walk round the room, in any direction, repeating the words quietly to themselves. On a given sound, e.g. a cymbal, each child stops walking, turns to the nearest person, and speaks the words with much expression, as if they are breaking some exciting news. The cymbal is played again, and the children immediately continue walking and return to saying the words quietly. Repeat the activity a few times.

Singing the good news

Now ask the children to sing the words (with or without the recording) using as much expression as they did when breaking the good news to a friend. They will need to have a bright smiley face, and use their eyes to help the words come alive. To help them to project their enthusiasm to the listener, they should:

- Sing in a slightly detached (bouncy) manner; this will be helped if the consonants are clearly articulated, especially:
  – 'Chr' of Christmas;
  – fat;
  – 'p' of please, put and penny;
  – old;
  – hat;
  – If;
  – 'h' of ha'penny;
  – God.
- Articulate all 's' sounds at the very last minute; avoid hissing snakes.
- There are two minim (half-note) beats in every bar. Make sure the singers are silent for exactly one beat at the end of each line.

Singing as a round

When the children are confidently singing in unison, and have mastered the rather tricky leaps (shown in boxes on the song sheet) in the melody line, divide them into three groups and ask them to sing the song as a round. If they are up for a challenge, ask them to sing the round whilst they all walk around the room in different directions.

Achievement

Can say and sing with expression. Can sing in the required style. Can understand how to use consonants to enhance expression and style. Can sing in a round. Can sing a round when not standing in a group.

Christmas is Coming

Traditional English round

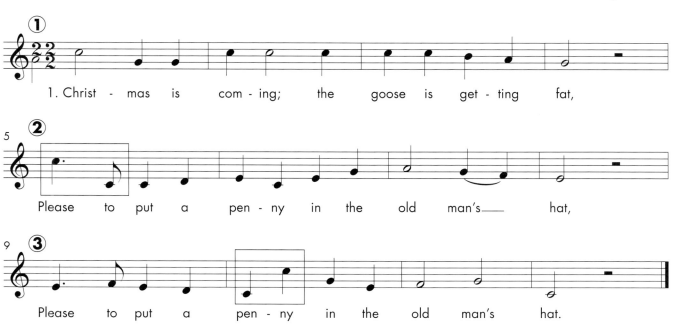

1. Christ - mas is com - ing; the goose is get - ting fat,

Please to put a pen - ny in the old man's___ hat,

Please to put a pen - ny in the old man's hat.

2. If you have no penny, a ha'penny will do;
   If you have no ha'penny, then God bless you,
   If you have no ha'penny, then God bless you.

CHAPTER 6

Sing what you mean

Lesson 3

Now Light One Thousand Christmas Lights

Focus

Deciding upon dynamics. Listening for, and performing with, a good blend and tonal quality. Extending the song.

Resources

CD 3 tracks 7, 8; song sheet 43.

About the song

A folk carol from Sweden.

Activities

The essentials

Play track 7 several times for the children to pick up the carol. Remind them about posture, about taking in the right amount of breath for each phrase and about giving each phrase a musical shape. Discuss the expression with the children and ask them to decide how best to include any dynamics in the carol.

Blend and tone

This is a very simple, short song which needs to be sung legato (smoothly) with a good blend and tonal quality. Without employing these singing skills, the carol will sound very ordinary and the simple flow and beauty of the melodic line will be lost. Revise this activity (first undertaken in Chapter 6 lesson 1). Use the song sheet or write the words of the first verse on the board and ask the children to underline or highlight the vowels. Listen to track 8. The singer is singing the words without any consonants. Play just one line and ask the children to copy the singer exactly. They will have to listen very carefully and should only move on to the next line when they understand what they are trying to accomplish. Practise this frequently, and with any other song to improve the vowels, the blend and the tonal quality.

Extension

This song is short and the children may like to think of ways in which it can be extended. For example you could:

- ask them all to sing the first verse;
- ask them all to hum as many 'verses' of the carol as required;
- ask for a volunteer to play the melody on a glockenspiel whilst the rest of the class hum;
- ask for some volunteers to say a poem or to read a short passage whilst the rest of the class hum; or
- sing the second verse.

Achievement

Can understand and employ dynamics sensitively. Can understand about blend, tone and unanimity of vowels. Can sing unanimous vowels. Can contribute to discussions on how to extend the carol.

Now Light One Thousand Christmas Lights

Folk song from Sweden

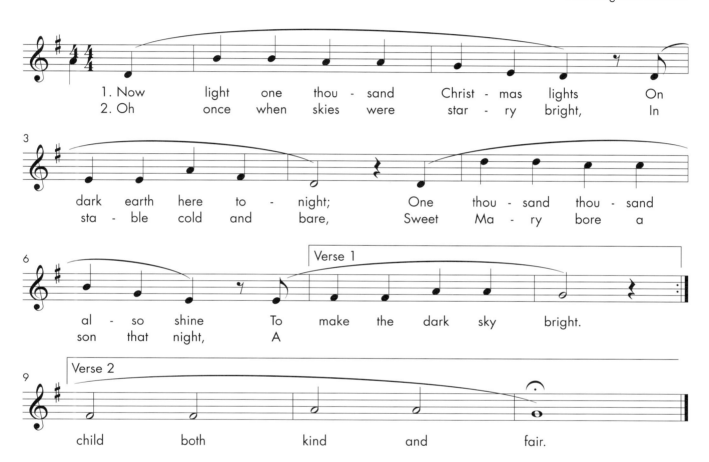

1. Now light one thou - sand Christ - mas lights On dark earth here to - night; One thou - sand thou - sand

2. Oh once when skies were star - ry bright, In sta - ble cold and bare, Sweet Ma - ry bore a

Verse 1
al - so shine To make the dark sky bright.
son that night, A

Verse 2
child both kind and fair.

CHAPTER 6

Sing what you mean

Lesson 4

Songs of the West (7)

Focus

Identifying important words. Recognising how musical features change the mood and add variety to a song. Deciding the best dynamics and expressive features. Singing a solo or singing in a small group.

Resources

CD 1 tracks 11, 12, 13, 14; song sheets 9, 10, 11, 12, 13 (pages 18–22).

About the song

Three traditional American folk songs. See Chapter 1 lesson 5.

Activities

Rock Island Line – speedy words and rolling tunes

Play track 11 and help the children to decide which are the most important words. (*Rock Island Line, mighty, ride it.*) Play the song again and challenge them to identify which words and musical features in the refrain give the feeling that the train is moving at speed. (*In the first three phrases, the words repeat and easily roll off the tongue. The melody is centred on one note, which incessantly drives its way forward to the last phrase. In the last, extra-long phrase, the percussive nature of the consonants imitates the fast rhythmic clickety-clack of the steam train. The melody rattles along circling around three notes (G E A), emphasising the easy movement of this train.*)

Midnight Special – repetition and texture

Play track 12. Focus the children's listening and ask them to identify the musical features that are used to increase the excitement with each repetition of the Midnight Special. (*Texture (the number of parts singing at any one time) and timbre (colour): the first refrain makes a unison statement, the second is in two parts and the third is in three parts.*)

Worried Man – changing moods

Play track 13 and ask the children if they can recognise the difference in the mood between the beginning and end of the song. (*It starts in a worried mood, but finishes in a brighter one.*) Challenge the children to identify the musical features that are used to change the mood. (*1st verse = solo man's voice with no embellishments and a simple accompaniment. 2nd verse = children's voices added; more instruments make a punchier backing and they lift the mood. 3rd verse = children only; the song moves up a key i.e. it is higher in pitch which adds excitement and anticipation; second vocal part uses high notes to add to the excitement; backing adds higher pitches, has a richer texture and a much stronger beat. The message is that the man really won't be worried long.*)

Now discuss with the children exactly what dynamics and expressive features they would like to include in the three Songs of the West songs. Are there volunteers for soloists (e.g. where the man sings), or small-group singing (e.g. the counter-melody or the third part)? Write the expression marks on the song sheets as an *aide memoire*. If you have a balance control you can use it to remove all the vocal parts from track 14, so the children can sing with the instrumental backing. By using suitable conducting gestures, help the children to follow all their chosen expression marks. Record the performance and let the children evaluate their work.

Achievement

Can identify important words. Can recognise how musical elements and features are used to change mood and add variety to a song. Can incorporate suitable dynamics and other expressive features. Can sing a solo or in a small group. Can evaluate their own work.

Sing what you mean

Lesson 5

Thank You For the Music

Focus

Understanding how a composer uses musical features to create the desired effect. Following the contour of a melody. Creating a dance routine. Presenting and performing.

Resources

CD 3 tracks 9, 10, 11; song sheets 44, 45.

About the song

One of the many highly successful songs from the Swedish pop group Abba.

Activities

Absorbing the song

Play track 9 at any appropriate time during the day e.g. during registration or break. The children will probably sing along (to themselves) with the recording and they will absorb the song and soon be able to sing it from memory.

The structure and melodic shape

Make a copy of the verse available for the children to see (the first page of the song sheet). Explain to them that the chatty style of the verse is like an introduction to the more 'up beat' refrain, just the same as an introduction to a story would be. The melody is pitched low i.e. in a similar register to that of the spoken voice. Play track 11 to the children and ask them to listen to the verse being spoken. Ask them to point to the notes as the words are spoken and to notice how the speaking voice moves up and down following the same contour (the direction in which the notes move) as the melodic line. Use your hand in the air to reflect the melodic contour, and ask the children to say the words of the verse making the pitch of their voices mirror the rise and fall of your hand.

The refrain

After the verse, there are pauses on three repeated notes ('So I say'), which lead into the highly catchy melody and strong beat of the refrain. The refrain is rhythmic, higher in pitch than the verse and drives on to the end of the song. If you have a balance control use it with tracks 10 and 9 to listen, separately, to the soloist, the children and the accompaniment. This song virtually sings itself, but just make sure that the children sing with joy and enthusiasm and not with their shouting voices. Projecting their voices to the back of the room will produce volume.

Dance

It is difficult to sing this song standing still! Ask the children to think of pop videos and to remember at least two of the moves that bands perform to their songs. Discuss their findings and ask for volunteers to demonstrate the moves they have remembered. Divide the children into small groups (four to six people) and challenge them to create their own dance sequence to go with the refrain. Remind them to keep the moves simple and to think about how they will flow smoothly from one to the next. The character of the moves will need to fit the character of the song; for instance, the moves are unlikely to be slow, minimal or gentle.

Allow each group to perform their dance whilst the rest of the class sings the song. Ask the children (both singers and dancers) to evaluate their own performances and to find ways of improving them.

Achievement

Can understand about the structure and the effective use of musical features. Can follow a melody line. Can create a dance routine. Can perform with good presentation skills. Can evaluate and improve.

SONG SHEET 44

Thank You for the Music

Benny Andersson and Bjorn Ulvaeus

Sounds of Singing Y5–6/P6–7 © Alison Ley, Nelson Thornes Ltd, 2004

Thank You for the Music (continued)

ask in all hon - es - ty,_____ What would life be?_____ With - out a song_

_____ or a dance, what are we?_____ So I say thank you for the mu - sic, for

1st and 2nd time | last time

giv - ing it to me._____ So I say giv - ing it to me.

Sounds of Singing Y5–6/P6–7 © Alison Ley, Nelson Thornes Ltd, 2004

CHAPTER 6

Sing what you mean

Lesson 6

We're Going to the Country

Focus

Identifying the character and expression of the song. Clapping the word rhythms. Accurately pitching notes. Singing with a different accent. Singing in two parts. Dramatising the story.

Resources

CD 3 tracks 12, 13; song sheets 46, 47.

About the song

This song comes from the musical *Blitz!*, written by Lionel Bart, a 20th-century British composer who is perhaps best remembered for the musical *Oliver!*

Activities

If you have a balance control, use it to play the just the instrumental backing on track 12 and ask the children what the music reminds them of (*they will probably say marching*). Discuss the evacuation of children from big cities to the country during the 1939–1945 war and how they might have felt excited at the prospect. The parents knew that the reality of evacuation was not exciting. Use the balance control with track 13 to play the parts of the children and the parents separately, and ask the children to describe the difference in the singing between the two parts. (*The children's voices are strong and confident; they are looking forward to living in the country. The parents' voices are shaky and at times really faltering as they begin to feel the heartbreak of saying goodbye to their children.*)

The first part (the children)

Play this part to the children and ask them to tap the rhythm of the melody along with the recording. Aim for precision and a good ensemble – no stray claps. When the rhythm is instilled, ask the children to first hum and then quietly sing the first part with the recording. They must listen carefully as this part moves in leaps and pitching the right note can be a problem. Make the words clear, rhythmic and strongly articulate the consonants. The children on the recording sing this with a stage 'London' accent. Help your children to hear the inflections and ask them to copy the accent with unison vowels.

The second part (the parents)

Learn the second part in the same way as the first – that is by clapping the rhythm and then humming the melody with the recording and finally singing the words in a stage 'London' accent with unified vowels.

If you have a balance control you can use it with the 'split vocals' recording to isolate this part.

The expression and singing in parts

Revise the meaning behind the song, and help the children to sing both parts (separately at this stage) with the appropriate expression. Before you divide the class for two-part singing, ask them to sing one part and play the other part on the recording. Only put the parts together when you are sure that the intonation, articulation, style and character of each part is really good.

Some children may like to dramatise the story of the song as the rest are singing. This would add yet more variety to the performance of an already challenging song.

Achievement

Can recognise the character and expression of the song. Can clap the word rhythms with precision. Can pitch the notes accurately. Can sing with unanimity of vowels in a stage 'London' accent. Can hold a part. Can dramatise the song.

We're Going to the Country

Words and music by Lionel Bart

SONG SHEET 47

We're Going to the Country (continued)

90

Sounds of Singing Y5–6/P6–7 © Alison Ley, Nelson Thornes Ltd, 2004

Attention to detail

This chapter concentrates on listening to the finer musical details and features (e.g. texture and dynamics) within a piece of music or in a song or in the backing of a song. It helps children to replicate those details with great precision, and to take account of them when they make decisions about how to interpret a song.

There is a song in Portuguese requiring careful listening in order to hear the inflections and pronunciation of another language.

There are opportunities to add some vocal improvisation over recorded song and to create a skiffle backing to a song. Further background information is given about the 1950s skiffle craze.

There are several activities that revolve around listening to word rhythms and copying them. Some rhythms are reasonably straightforward, whilst others are quite demanding. Inner hearing is developed through working with syncopated rhythms and there is also a chance to invent rhythm patterns to fit into a song.

There are three part-songs, and performing and presentation skills are revised.

Lesson	Focus
El Concierto	Listening to other languages
	Copying accents and inflections
	Singing in a foreign accent
	Singing robustly
	Putting a pattern in a space
Fishing	Understanding when to end a note
	Dealing with diphthongs
	Rehearsing and performing in groups
	Improvising scat patterns
Mistletoe and Wine	Playing 'Rhythm Switch'
	Listening for texture and dynamics
	Performing and presenting
Songs of the West (8)	Changing the style of a song
	Learning about skiffle
	Creating a skiffle backing track
	Singing with their skiffle backing
Syncopation	Identifying syncopated rhythms
	Clapping and chanting with good ensemble
	Singing in the appropriate style
	Singing in two parts
	Creating moves

CHAPTER 7

Attention to detail

Lesson 1

El Concierto

Focus

Listening to other languages. Copying accents and inflections. Singing in a foreign accent. Singing robustly. Putting a pattern in a space.

Resources

CD 3 tracks 14, 15, 16; song sheet 48.

About the song

A folk song from Brazil.

Activities

Other languages

Play track 14 and ask the children to listen very carefully to these phrases:

1) *Chacun à son goût* (French – everyone to his taste).
2) *Borgen macht sorgen* (German – borrowing makes sorrowing).
3) *Gli asseti hanno torto* (Italian – the absent are in the wrong).
4) *Exempla sunt odiosa* (Latin – examples are hateful).

After each phrase, pause the recording and ask the children to copy the speaker's voice exactly – the inflection (the different pitches within each word) and the tone of the voice. Explain that each phrase is in a different language and that each language has its own particular inflection and sound. German is somewhat guttural, French has a nasal quality, Italian is light and lilting, and Latin has no diphthongs (vowel mixtures) so has a pure and open sound.

Singing in another language

Play El Concierto (track 15) to the children and ask them to guess what language is being sung (*Brazilian Portugese*). If you have a balance control, isolate the vocals so that you can hear the pronunciation of the words more clearly. To achieve the right mood and character for the song, help the children to replicate the accent precisely. They will have to work overtime with their lips, tongues and teeth to project the words clearly. Practise saying them slowly with lots of rolled 'r's and exaggerated consonants; then sing them slowly (unaccompanied) and finally sing them up to speed with the recorded backing.

Singing quality

The children will have noticed that the singing on the recording is robust, loud and lively – just as if they were singing in the open air at a carnival or at some other celebration. Explain that Brazil is home to some of the best carnivals in the world. Encourage them to sing this song in an energetic and boisterous manner. They may want to use their 'shouting' (belt) voice for this, which is appropriate as long as it is not over-loud and unmusical.

Put a pattern in space

Listen to track 16. A different tapping rhythm has been added at the end of each phrase. Ask the children to make up their own rhythms, either using the same rhythm throughout, or a number of different ones. Ask for volunteers to clap their rhythm (or play it on a percussion instrument) whilst the rest of the class sing the song.

Achievement

Can hear and replicate foreign language texts. Can sing in another accent. Can sing robustly. Can put a pattern in a space.

SONG SHEET 48

El Concierto

Folk song from Brazil

Tu - bas, trom - pe - tas, trom - bo - nes

Los sa - xó - fo - nes con el flau - tín,

El cla - ri - net - te y el bom - bo

Hoy - nos brin - dan un ra - to

1. fe - liz.   2. liz. ¡O - lé!

Sounds of Singing Y5–6/P6–7 © Alison Ley, Nelson Thornes Ltd, 2004

CHAPTER 7

Attention to detail

Lesson 2

Fishing

Focus

Understanding when to end a note. Dealing with diphthongs. Rehearsing and performing in groups. Improvising scat patterns.

Resources

CD 3 tracks 17, 18, 19, 20; song sheets 49, 50.

About the song

This is a folk song from Greece.

Activities

Breathing

Begin the lesson with some deep, low breathing exercises (see 'All about warm-ups' page xviii and Chapter 1 lessons 3, 4 and 6) to prepare the children for the long phrases in this song.

The refrain

Hand out or project the lyrics, or write the words of the refrain on the board. Play track 17 and help the children to notice that the refrain is sung in two parts, with the second echoing the first phrase by phrase. Ask the children to sing the echo as soon as they feel able. Play the song again, and this time divide the class in two with one half singing the first part and the other half singing the echo. The echo must be quieter than the first part. Watch out for the following tricky bits:

- Hold each long note on for the full count of four, i.e. sing until you reach the fifth note when you stop: $1\rightarrow2\rightarrow3\rightarrow4\rightarrow$off.
- Dee - - - - - - - p.
- Put the last consonant of 'deep', 'bite' and 'might' actually on the fifth beat.
- Listen to track 19 to hear how the difficult vowels on the long notes should be pronounced. The singer sings each one incorrectly the first time, then correctly.

Performing the verse

Divide the class into small groups. Throughout the week make the recording available so that each group can teach themselves one of the verses from the song. During the next few lessons hear each group sing their verse whilst the rest of the class sings the refrain. Ask the class to appraise each other's work, giving praise for breathing in the right places, for good diction, intonation and presentation skills.

Improvising

Play track 20 and ask the children to describe what the singer is doing (*improvising, using scat words*). Play track 18 and ask the children to walk around the room in any direction and to improvise in the same way, quietly singing to themselves. If you have a balance control, use it to remove the echo part from the refrain. The children may find it easier to hear themselves if they put a finger in one ear as they sing. Once they begin to tune in to this exercise and feel a degree of confidence, ask them to sing in several different ways: like an opera singer, as if they were in the bath, on the top of a hill, singing down the telephone, etc.

Achievement

Can understand and perform held notes correctly. Can pronounce diphthongs correctly. Can learn and rehearse in groups without help. Can perform in a group. Can improvise over a given chord structure.

Fishing

Folk song from Greece
English words by Nick Curtis

SONG SHEET 50

Fishing (continued)

English words by Nick Curtis

Refrain

In the ocean deep,
Out in the ocean blue,
Fishes come and go,
Just like me and you.

Hope to get a bite,
Catch one if I might.
Nothing much to do,
Out in the ocean blue.

Sounds of Singing Y5–6/P6–7 © Alison Ley, Nelson Thornes Ltd, 2004

Attention to detail

Lesson 3

Mistletoe and Wine

Focus

Playing 'Rhythm Switch'. Listening for texture and dynamics. Performing and presenting.

Resources

CD 3 tracks 21, 22, 23; song sheets 51, 52.

About the song

A song made popular in the UK by Cliff Richard.

Activities

Singing in phrases

Play track 21 several times. Ask the children to join in the refrain as soon as they feel confident. Breathe at the end of the phrases, which are marked on the song sheet.

Texture and dynamics

Ask the children to listen carefully to the backing track (if you have a balance control use it to isolate the backing track) and to notice how the texture (number of instruments playing at any one time) and the dynamics increase with each refrain. When they sing, they should make the expression and dynamics of each refrain slightly different from the previous one.

Playing Rhythm Switch

Familiarise the children with the Mistletoe and Wine rhythm patterns on song sheet 52. Project or write them up so everyone can see them. Clap through them several times – it may help to say the words at the same time. Next, point to the patterns in random order, giving the class time to clap each one at least four times before switching. (The rhythm patterns are recorded on track 23 just for reference, but it is important that you clap them yourself with the class.)

Now arrange the children in a large circle and remove the rhythm pattern notation (so they have to listen more carefully with no visual cues). You clap any one of the eight different rhythm patterns several times, asking the class to join in when they have 'caught' the pattern. While the children are copying your last pattern, say 'switch' and clap a different pattern. The class joins in again with the new pattern. Do not break the steady beat as you change to each new pattern. In other words, the children have to clap one pattern at the same time as listening to you clap a new one. When they can do this successfully, ask for volunteers to be a leader. This game can be played with any rhythm patterns and with different metres: three beats (tap, clap, clap) or four beats in a bar (tap, clap, clap, clap).

Performing and presenting

Ask for volunteers, or select your best singers, to sing the verses as solos. The rest of the children sing the refrain. Perform the song to an audience and ask the class to imagine they are singing to one person who is right at the back of the hall. Establish happy faces, joyful singing, enthusiasm, good posture, but a flexible stance. You may like to revise the 'Breaking the news' activity in Chapter 6 lesson 2. If the song is going to be received well, it is important to rehearse all these presentation skills until they are second nature – especially the smiles.

Achievement

Can clap a rhythm pattern and listen to a different one at the same time. Can understand the use of texture and dynamics. Can demonstrate good use of performance and presentation skills.

SONG SHEET 51

Mistletoe and Wine

Words by Leslie Stewart and Jeremy Paul
Music by Keith Strachan

1. The child is a king, the carollers sing,
    The old is past, there's a new beginning.
    Dreams of Santa, dreams of snow,
    Fingers numb, faces aglow. It's. . .

2. A time for living, a time for believing,
    A time for trusting, not deceiving.
    Love and laughter and joy ever after;
    Ours for the taking, just follow the master.

3. It's a time for giving, a time for getting,
    A time for forgiving, and for forgetting.
    Christmas is love, Christmas is peace;
    A time for hating and fighting to cease.

Sounds of Singing Y5–6/P6–7 © Alison Ley, Nelson Thornes Ltd, 2004

Mistletoe and Wine Rhythm Patterns

CHAPTER 7

Attention to detail

Lesson 4

Songs of the West (8)

Focus

Changing the style of a song. Learning about skiffle. Creating a skiffle backing track. Singing with their skiffle backing.

Resources

CD 1 tracks 25, 14; untuned percussion instruments and keyboard (optional); song sheets 9–13 (pages 18–22).

About the music

Three traditional American folk songs. See Chapter 1 lesson 5.

'Skiffle' music has its roots in the blues and folk idioms. It was a term describing the replacement of 'trad jazz' instruments with (low-cost) washboards for percussion, tea-chest-and-broom-handle-bass, guitar and kazoo. It emerged in Britain in the 1950s when Lonnie Donegan (who became known as the King of Skiffle) formed his skiffle band. Skiffle preceded the rock'n'roll of Elvis Presley and Chuck Berry but it was the subsequent influence and combination of all these styles, and the apparent ease with which anyone could have a go, that inspired thousands of teenagers to form bands. Skiffle's time in the limelight was short, and its successful exponents could be counted on the fingers of one hand, but its influence on popular music was hugely disproportionate. It almost literally put guitars into the hands of a generation of teenagers who went on to create the British pop and rock scene of the 1960s.

Activities

About skiffle

Explain about skiffle music. The children might research it on the internet or in the library. Listen to the recording of Lonnie Donegan's skiffle group playing Don't You Rock Me Daddy-O (track 25). Talk about the mood of the music; what does it make the children feel?

Home-grown skiffle band

Ask the children to suggest which instruments they could use to make their own skiffle-band percussion section. (*Any of the following: metal guiro or cabassa to replace the washboard; comb and paper to replace kazoo; possibly a tambourine, or hi-hat cymbal and a guitar.*)

Chord sequence

The chord sequence (see Chapter 4, lesson 4) in Songs of the West is very simple and, like most skiffle music, it uses only two or three chords. If you have a guitar or a keyboard, play the chord symbols printed on the song sheets, or play them using the 'single finger' chord facility. If you do not have a keyboard, use track 14 (if you have a balance control, play the backing track only). Ask the children to decide where and when they could use their percussion instruments as an accompaniment to the song. Revise the third activity in chapter 6 lesson 4, which looks at the backing arrangements in some detail, and encourage the children to arrange their percussion backing to complement both the vocals and the instrumental backing and not to overpower it. Remember that less is often more.

Singing with the skiffle backing track

When the children are satisfied with their backing arrangement, record it, as this will enable you to divide the class into 'parts' and to sing Songs of the West accompanied by their own home-grown backing track.

Achievement

Can sing and play in a different style. Can create a skiffle backing track to either stand on its own, or to complement a pre-recorded backing track.

Attention to detail

Syncopa-tion

Focus

Identifying syncopated rhythms. Clapping and chanting with good ensemble. Singing in the appropriate style. Singing in two parts. Creating moves.

Resources

CD 3 tracks 24, 25, 26; song sheet 53.

About the song

A specially written children's song by the British composer George Odam.

Activities

Identifying syncopated rhythms

Play track 24 and ask the children to listen for the 'syncopated' rhythms (those rhythms that place a strong emphasis on the weak or off-beat). These occur all through the song, but most obviously in section A, where there is a rest (silence) on the first strong beat of every bar and in section B over the word 'syncopation'.

Clapping the rests

This song is in the style of the 'swing' music of the 1930s, which originated in the USA. Note the American accent and, whilst engaging in the following activities, help the children to copy that accent. Play track 26 and ask them to listen to the lyrics being spoken in the rhythm of the words. Notice that a tambourine is played every time a rest occurs. Listen to the warm-up again, and ask the children to clap on the rest, but to say the words silently in their heads. Do this several times until everyone is clapping exactly on the first beat of every bar in section A, and on all the rests in sections B and C. Now do the same again, but ask the children to whisper the words really clearly, and to clap the rests. Finally repeat the exercise with the children saying the words out loud. Let the words trip lightly off the tongue, not laboured and heavy. Work on the 'ensemble', encouraging them to listen to each other and to all speak as one unit, not as a class of individuals.

Singing with rhythmic accuracy and style

Play track 24 and let the children clap on the rests. Repeat this until they have heard the melody enough times to be able to sing the song. Section A has an urgency about it – the melody is lively and bouncy. Section B has a contrasting legato (smooth) section to it. Section C is the coda (the tailpiece) and keeps repeating the note C, pushing us on to the last two bars which have no rests, and therefore no stops, and hurrying us to the end.

Two-part singing

Divide the class in two – group 1 and group 2.

Everyone sings sections A and B through once.

Group 1 sings section A, section B and section C.

Group 2 comes in with section A just as group 1 starts to sing section B.

Group 2 goes straight from section A to section C.

Movement

This is a great song to move to. Ask the children to think of some simple but very rhythmic moves that will reflect the syncopated melody.

Achievement

Can identify syncopated rhythms. Can clap and chant listening to others. Can sing in the appropriate style. Can sing in two parts. Can move rhythmically to the music.

SONG SHEET 53

Syncopation

Words and music by George Odam

Sounds of Singing Y5–6/P6–7 © Alison Ley, Nelson Thornes Ltd, 2004

Move it!

This chapter is about creating movement and dance to reflect the mood and character of the song or music. This relationship between music and movement is an invaluable tool when it comes to interpreting a song.

Some of the movement literally acts out the story of the song, whilst other lessons use the backing tracks as the starting point for drama, movement and celebration dances. Some movement is precise and very structured, whilst other movement allows much more freedom. All movement develops directly from the mood and structure of the music or the song.

There are ideas for celebrating the festival of Diwali. There are opportunities to create a television advert or a scene from a silent film.

There are opportunities to create dances and to sing songs in vastly differing styles. The work is done either as a whole-class activity, or in groups of about 5 or 6.

Lesson	Focus
The World Keeps Turning Around	Identifying repeats
	Singing a counter-melody
	Adding movement
Diwali Song	Learning about Diwali
	Singing a call and response song
	Responding to the mood of a song
	Creating a dance for presentation
Songs of the West (9)	Inventing dance moves to enhance a performance of Songs of the West
	Recording dance moves on paper
	Evaluating their own work
	Performing and presenting
River, River	Listening in detail to the mood and structure of a piece of music
	Creating an advertisement or a scene from a silent film
	Recording and appraising their work
	Performing and presenting
Winter Wonderland	Assessing the mood of the song
	Matching movement to lyrics
	Evaluating their own and others' work
	Combining work for a class performance

CHAPTER 8

Move it!

Lesson 1

The World Keeps Turning Around

Focus

Identifying repeats. Singing a counter-melody. Adding movement.

Resources

CD 3 tracks 27, 28; song sheets 54, 55.

About the song

A good song for assembly or a concert.

Activities

Identifying the repeats

Hand out or project the song sheets and play track 27. Help the children to recognise the many repeated musical features in this song:

- The first three lines have very similar melodies.
- The first three lines repeat their words.
- The fourth line repeats 'As the big wide world keeps turning around'.
- The words of the refrain are very repetitious.
- The melody (1st part) of the refrain mainly consists of short four-note phrases, which are linked together by the counter-melody (2nd part).
- The last line of the refrain is the same as the fourth line.

Singing the song

When the children have heard the song several times ask them to join in with the recording. Sing through each line of the verses – i.e. do not take a breath until the end of the line. If you have a balance control, use it with track 28 to teach one vocal part at a time, then divide the class in two and put both parts together.

Preparing to move

Energise the children by doing five minutes of physical warm-ups.

Spice it up

This is a great song, but because it is so well known it could, in performance, become very ordinary leaving the audience feeling that they have not had a very inspiring or uplifting experience. To spice it up a bit, ask the children to invent some moves that enhance the mood and presentation. Encourage them to let their moves reflect all the repetitions, but warn against making them too literal as that will look as if they are hamming it up. The movement for the first three lines of the verse could be exactly the same, but the very fact that the words are repeated implies that the writer is trying to emphasise a point. So, maybe the moves could become successively bigger, or more people could join in for each repetition. The refrain could include stillness where the silences occur in both parts, or it could just include relaxed clapping in appropriate places. Do not forget that the melody of the last line of both the verse and the refrain are exactly the same. Either the whole class can perform the moves, or a small group can perform whilst the rest of the class sings.

Achievement

Can identify repeats. Can sing and counter-melody. Can invent sympathetic moves that enhance the quality of the performance.

The World Keeps Turning Around

Words and music by Sue Stevens

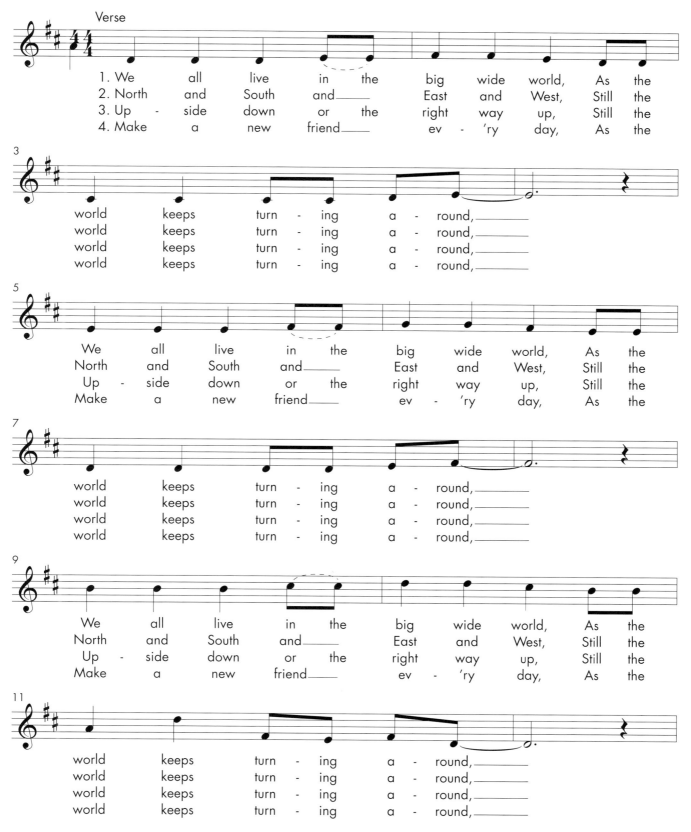

SONG SHEET 55

The World Keeps Turning Around
(continued)

Sounds of Singing Y5–6/P6–7 © Alison Ley, Nelson Thornes Ltd, 2004

CHAPTER 8

Move it!

Lesson 2

Diwali Song

Focus

Learning about Diwali. Singing a call and response song. Responding to the mood of a song. Creating a dance for presentation.

Resources

CD 3 tracks 29, 30; song sheet 56.

About the song

A song to celebrate Diwali.

Activities

About Diwali

Diwali is a Hindu festival of light and joy, where people from all age groups participate in festivities to give expression to their happiness. They light earthen diyas, decorate their houses, burst fire crackers and invite their friends and relations to their household for sumptuous feasts of sweets, and other special Diwali food. In the northern part of India, Diwali is celebrated as the return of Rama, along with Sita and Lakshman, from his fourteen-year exile after killing Ravana. To commemorate his return to Ayadhya, his subjects illuminated the kingdom and burst crackers.

Researching the customs and story

You may wish to set this lesson in the context of work in other subject areas, research into Diwali customs and the children's own experiences of Diwali. The work could be combined with a more extended project on Diwali, such as enacting the story of Sita and Rama. The song and dance could be used as the link between different aspects of the project.

Creating a dance

Play track 29, and help the children to learn both the call and response. Keep the singing legato and calm, and try to inject a quality of wonder. Ask for volunteers to sing the call whilst the rest of the class sings the response. If you have a balance control, play the backing track on its own and ask the children to listen carefully to the mood and texture of the accompaniment. Create a dance describing the mood of the song and of the accompaniment. The children could extend the music by singing the song, playing the accompaniment then repeating the song. Alternatively, they could play the accompaniment, sing the song, then play the accompaniment again.

Assessment

Can research the context of a song. Can sing a call and response song, capturing the mood. Can respond to the mood of a song by creating a dance. Can dance with good presentation skills.

SONG SHEET 56

Diwali Song

George Odam

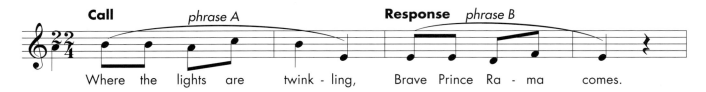

Where the lights are twink-ling, Brave Prince Ra - ma comes.

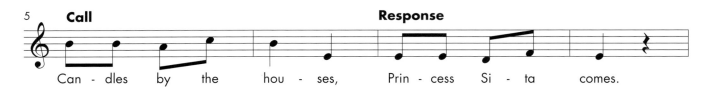

Can - dles by the hou - ses, Prin - cess Si - ta comes.

From the dark - ness Brave Prince Ra - ma comes.

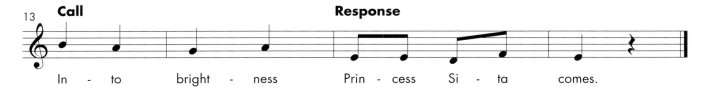

In - to bright - ness Prin - cess Si - ta comes.

108

Move it!

Songs of the West (9)

Focus

Inventing dance moves to enhance a performance of Songs of the West. Recording dance moves on paper. Evaluating their own work. Performing and presenting.

Resources

CD 1 tracks 14, 15.

About the song

Three traditional American folk songs. See Chapter 1 lesson 5.

Activities

Inventing movement

Gospel, trad jazz, skiffle, rock'n'roll, and subsequent popular music styles are great music for dancing. As we have seen from the other lessons that focus on Songs of the West, each of the three individual songs has its own mood, arrangement and character, even though they all have the same tempo and beat. The challenge is to invent some dance movements that will enhance those differences whilst not detracting from the song or completely distracting an audience from the singers.

Points to think about

Working with the whole class, guide and help the children to work out their moves and ask them to think about:

- creating different movements for different sections of a song – e.g. verse, refrain.
- creating the same movements for repeated sections.
- adding new movements with each new voice entry, when singing in parts.
- creating simple movements for the whole choir to perform whilst singing.
- adding an instrumental interlude for a separate group to perform some rock'n'roll or jive moves (they could use the backing track they created in Chapter 7 lesson 4, or the backing track on the recording).
- keeping the movements all the same size.
- keeping the movements exactly together with the beat.
- not dancing energetically at the same time as singing, as breathing will be compromised. Remember that modern pop bands do not often dance and sing at the same time. Usually they dance whilst miming the vocals to a recording of the song. Try that.
- getting ideas from films with rock'n'roll singers performing, e.g. *Summer Holiday* or *Grease*.
- getting ideas from films with gospel singers, as their moves are rhythmic, energetic, but at the same time very relaxed, e.g. as in the film *Sister Act*.
- finding a way of recording their dance moves on paper.
- not being afraid to change their plans and decisions in the light of critical evaluation.

Performance

When the singing and dancing is slick and highly polished, find an opportunity to perform the Songs of the West to a wider audience. If, by now, you have covered all the Songs of the West lessons that are featured in this book, the children will have worked very hard over a long period of time, on one set of songs. They will have a depth of knowledge about singing technique, and about the songs themselves, which should be of value to them when they sing and study other songs. Their final performance and presentation of this song should be truly outstanding.

Achievement

Can work with others to invent sympathetic dance moves for Songs of the West. Can record their moves on paper. Can evaluate their own work. Can present and perform a song and dance routine.

Move it!

Lesson 4

River, River

Focus

Listening in detail to the mood and structure of a piece of music. Creating an advertisement or a scene from a silent film. Recording and appraising their work. Performing and presenting.

Resources

CD 3 tracks 31, 32; song sheet 57.

About the song

A good 'sing along' song.

Activities

Listen to the instrumentals

Play the children the instrumental music on track 31. (This is the backing track to the song River, River, but at this stage do not play the song or tell the children what it is called.) Talk about the music and listen for the different instrumentation and the changes that occur as the piece progresses. (*There is a honky-tonk piano, a bass guitar, some clapping/tambourine sounds on the off-beat and a pizzicato (plucked, short) slightly funky sound. Towards the end there is a sound like a Hawaiian guitar.*) Listen to this several times so that the children have a chance to internalise the music and feel and recognise the structure (*two verses, refrain, interlude; two verses, refrain, interlude; two verses, refrain, refrain*).

Film or advertisement

Organise the children into groups of four to six. Ask them to imagine that the music they have just heard is the backing for either a silent movie or a TV advert. They have to create a scene from the film or think of a product that they wish to advertise, and use the music as their backing track. Explain about the pianist or organist creating the mood for the silent movie. Such people could make or break a film; jolly music during a tragic scene would be totally unacceptable. The changes in this music are quite subtle so the storyline does not have to be earth shattering as it does not swoop from comedy to tragedy. The music in TV adverts often says much more than the words. Could this be an advert for dog food, a car, or a day trip on the river?

Recording the work

Suggest that the children find some way of recording their work so that, when they resume next time, they will remember the stage they have reached. Allow plenty of time for this project so that the children can respond to the music in their most imaginative and creative manner.

Performing and presenting

When the projects are complete, ask the groups to perform their work to the rest of the class. You or they could video their efforts. When each group has performed, ask them to appoint a spokesperson who will explain to the class how they set about creating their scene and what they were thinking about when they listened to the music. Let everyone evaluate each other's work, giving plenty of praise and perhaps some useful constructive criticism.

Singing the song

Now listen to the song River, River on track 32. This is an easy song to pick up, so teach it by rote and just enjoy singing it.

Achievement

Can listen and internalise the mood and structure of a piece of music. Can create, record, perform and present their project. Can appraise their own and others' work.

River, River

Words and music by Peter Combe

2. Fishes they swim, swim in the river (x3)
   Catch one for my tea.

   Refrain

3. Wind blow cold at the top of the mountain (x3)
   Cold as the wind can be.

4. Skies are grey and the rain falling (x3)
   Pitter patter down on me.

   Refrain

5. Sun comes up and shines on the river (x3)
   Such a pretty sight to see.

6. Sun goes down and it's dark on the mountain (x3)
   Dark as the night can be.

   Refrain

   Refrain

CHAPTER 8

Move it!

Lesson 5

Winter Wonder-land

Focus

Assessing the mood of the song. Matching movement to lyrics. Evaluating their own and others' work. Combining work for a class performance.

Resources

CD 3 tracks 33, 34; song sheet 58.

About the song

A popular song from the USA.

Activities

Creating the right mood

Play track 34 and ask the children to listen to the images that the words create. Discuss with them the mood of the song (*lively, happy, fun*). Teach them both parts of the song and sing it with a lively and jaunty swing.

Matching movements to words

Divide the class into four groups. Allocate each group one verse giving them a copy of the words. Ask them to think of some movements that can be performed as the song is being sung. The movements must be simple and rhythmic, and should enhance the song, not detract from it – don't ham it up too much! Once the children are very familiar with the song you can use track 33 with the balance control, if you have one, to play the backing only, so they can practise their movements without the words. They will need to be able to hear the melody line in their heads (inner hearing). Watch each group and look for good movement co-ordination and ensemble.

Performing to each other

Ask each group to sing and dance their verse to the rest of the class. Ask the children to evaluate each other's performances. They should look at the 'ensemble', the facial expressions (do they look happy?), the appropriateness of the chosen movements, the presentation (are they engaging the audience?) and the quality of the singing (can the words be heard – are they singing in tune?). Ask each group how they think they may be able to improve their own work and ask the class for some helpful suggestions.

Whole-class performance

After all four groups have presented their movements, select just one group's movement, for everyone to perform, on the last line of every verse. Present this song with the whole class on a special occasion. Simple co-ordination of clothes (perhaps jeans and bright t-shirts) will have a very positive visual effect.

Assessment

Can assess the mood of a song. Can imaginatively create movement to reflect lyrics. Can positively evaluate their own and other's work. Can work in a large group for a whole-class performance.

Winter Wonderland

Music by Felix Bernard
Words by Dick Smith

(A) Sleighbells ring, are you listening?
In the lane snow is glistening,
A beautiful sight, we're happy tonight,
Walking in a winter wonderland!

(A) Gone away is the bluebird,
Here to stay is a new bird,
He's singing a song as we go along,
Walking in a winter wonderland!

[B] In the meadow we can build a snowman,
And pretend that he's a circus clown,
We'll have lots of fun with Mister Snowman,
Until the other kiddies knock him down!

(A) When is snows, ain't it thrilling?
Though your nose gets a chilling,
We'll frolic and play the Eskimo way
Walking in a winter wonderland!

Songs of the West Overview

Any song we sing requires a multitude of skills to make it sound not merely good but outstanding. The nine individual Songs of the West lessons in this book build into a project devoted to covering all the skills that go towards creating a satisfyingly outstanding performance.

Songs of the West is an arrangement for children's voices of three traditional American folksongs. Railroad men and hobos (travelling workers) were the heroes of many such songs in the 1930s and 1940s. The railroad itself was an important symbol to Americans and was more than just a means of transport – it also meant freedom and opportunity.

Rock Island Line

The Rock Island Railway Line was built between 1851 and 1854 and connected Chicago to Rock Island on the Mississippi River in Illinois. Kelly Pace, a prisoner in Arkansas, wrote this song in about 1934. Huddie 'Leadbelly' Ledbetter, the black American folk singer (died 1949), made a phonograph recording of the song. In 1955, Lonnie Donegan heard the recording and made his own arrangement of the song for guitar, bass and washboard. That song was the start of the 'skiffle' craze that swept across Britain and the USA.

Midnight Special

This traditional American folksong was collected from a Texas jail in about 1933. The lyrics used in Songs of the West are those of the refrain.

Worried Man

This is a traditional Hillbilly song. Hillbillies lived simple lives in the Appalachian mountain regions of the south-eastern United States. Hillbilly folksongs are widely sung today and appeal to people because they are hybrid songs with European, African-American and urban popular song influences.

Chapter	Lesson		Focus
Songs of the West (1)	1	5	Introducing a project on Songs of the West Learning about the origins of the songs Learning about the lyrics
Songs of the West (2)	1	6	Taking deep breaths Learning the melody line Taking quick breaths Singing through phrases
Songs of the West (3)	2	4	Identifying and performing a different accent Inventing and performing a patter-sentence Evaluating their own progress Achieving accuracy, precision and clarity of diction
Songs of the West (4)	3	4	Recognising and understanding how 'popular' (jazz, swing, pop and rock) rhythms are written and performed. Recognising a canon Learning a harmony part Putting two parts together
Songs of the West (5)	4	3	Recognising and singing a chord sequence Singing in three parts Recognising and identifying structures
Songs of the West (6)	5	4	Opening the mouth 'north-south' Learning how to sing high notes Singing in two parts

Chapter	Lesson		Focus
Songs of the West (7)	6	4	Identifying important words Recognising how musical features change the mood and add variety to a song Deciding the best dynamics and expressive features Singing a solo or singing in a small group
Songs of the West (8)	7	4	Changing the style of a song Learning about skiffle Creating a skiffle backing track Singing with their skiffle backing
Songs of the West (9)	8	3	Inventing dance moves to enhance a performance of Songs of the West Recording dance moves on paper Evaluating their own work Performing and presenting

Resources

The relevant song sheets and information sheets are printed adjacent to the lessons where they are first introduced. When they are referred to in subsequent lessons, page references are given to make it easy to locate the sheets quickly. You may like to photocopy the song sheets so you can always have them in front of you.

Sheet	Page	Contents
Song sheet 7	15	Rock Island Line and Midnight Special lyrics
Song sheet 8	16	Worried Man lyrics
Song sheet 9	18	Rock Island Line notation and lyrics
Song sheets 10-11	19-20	Midnight Special notation and lyrics
Song sheets 12-13	21-22	Worried Man notation and lyrics
Song sheet 18	33	Songs of the West Patter

The recordings used for the Songs of the West lessons are all placed together on CD 1. This means that you won't have to change CDs during a lesson.

CD/track	Title
1/14	Songs of the West complete
1/15	Songs of the West complete (split vocals)
1/11	Rock Island Line
1/18	Rock Island Line (split vocals)
1/19	Rock Island Line (new version)
1/12	Midnight Special
1/20	Midnight Special (split vocals)
1/22	Midnight Special (third part)
1/13	Worried Man
1/24	Worried Man (split vocals)
1/17	Songs of the West Patter 1
1/17	Songs of the West Patter 2 (fast)
1/17	Songs of the West Patter 3 (getting faster)
1/16	Breathing exercise
1/21	Three parts warm-up
1/23	High notes warm-up
1/25	Don't You Rock Me Daddy-O

Correlations

Singing is universal. While there may be differences of expression in the curriculum requirements and guidelines of different countries, in essence they are much the same and it is this common purpose that forms the basis of *Sounds of Singing*.

At the time of going to print, *Sounds of Singing* has been correlated to the following documents:

- National Curriculum 2000 (England)

- DfES/QCA Scheme of Work for Key Stages 1 and 2 Music (England)

- Music in the National Curriculum in Wales

- Expressive Arts 5–14 (Scotland)

These correlations may be viewed or downloaded free of charge from our Web site, www.nelsonthornes.com/soundsofsinging

The Northern Ireland Curriculum is under review at the time of writing. A correlation will be made as soon as possible.

All curriculum guidelines and requirements are subject to change, so please visit the Web site for updated correlation charts.

If you have difficulty accessing the Internet, hard copies of the correlations are available, also free of charge, from your Nelson Thornes representative or from our offices. Please telephone 01242 267280.

Sounds of Music

Sounds of Singing has been designed so that it may be used to complement *Sounds of Music*, providing a focused singing course. Many of the songs and listening extracts are common to both programmes, but all the lessons, activities and warm-ups in *Sounds of Singing* are new. If you wish to co-ordinate your use of the two schemes, the information below will help you to plan. You may also wish to use the *Repertoire in Sounds of Singing Y5–6/P6–7* in helping you to select content from *Sounds of Singing* to support your general music scheme of work.

Music also used in *Sounds of Music Y5/P6*

Christmas is Coming
Coffee Round, The
Ebony Trousers
El Concierto
Everybody's Got a Little Rhythm
Fishing
Gossip
Matilda
Syntax Error
Termite, The
Vesper Hymn
World Keeps Turning Around, The

Music also used in *Sounds of Music Y6/P7*

Diwali Song
Dona Nobis Pacem
Good News
Mistletoe and Wine
Notin' Around
Now Light One Thousand Christmas Lights
Silver Moon
Song for Oxum
Songs of the West
Syncopation
Thank You for the Music
Turn, Turn, Turn
We're Going to the Country
White Cliffs of Dover, The
Work-a-day Mornin' Blues
You'll Never Walk Alone

Repertoire in Sounds of Singing Y5-6/P6-7

Songs and chants

	chapter	lesson	page	origin
Christmas is Coming	6	2	80	Traditional round (Britain)
Coffee Round, The	2	1	26	Traditional round (Europe)
Diwali Song	8	2	108	Indian style
Dona Nobis Pacem	2	3	31	Traditional round (Latin)
Ebony Trousers	1	1	4–5	Nonsense round (Switzerland)
El Concierto	7	1	93	Traditional (Brazil)
Evening Prayer	5	1	64–5	Opera (Germany)
Everybody's Got a Little Rhythm	3	1	37	Children's song (Australia)
Fishing	7	2	95–6	Traditional (Greece)
Geordie's Penker	4	2	52	Traditional (Britain)
Good News	3	5	45–6	Gospel (USA)
Gossip	4	1	49–50	Composed round (Britain)
Jikel 'Emaweni	4	2	53	Traditional (South Africa)
Matilda	5	2	67	Traditional calypso (Caribbean)
Midnight Special	1	5	19–20	Traditional (USA)
Mistletoe and Wine	7	3	98	Popular (Britain)
Notin' Around	5	3	69–70	Children's song (Britain)
Now Light One Thousand Christmas Lights	6	3	83	Traditional (Sweden)
Ritti-ritti Soundscape	1	1	6	Sound picture
River, River	8	4	111	Children's song (Australia)
Rock Island Line	1	5	18	Traditional (USA)
Silver Moon	3	2	39–40	Traditional
Song for Oxum	4	5	61	Traditional (Brazil)
Songs of the West	1	5	14	Folk song arrangement (USA)
Syncopation	7	5	102	Children's song (Britain)
Syntax Error	2	2	28–9	Children's song (Australia)
Thank You for the Music	6	5	86–7	Popular (Sweden)
Termite, The	1	2	8	Chant (USA)
Turn, Turn, Turn	5	5	74	Popular folk (USA)
Vesper Hymn	6	1	78–9	Traditional (Europe)
We're Going to the Country	6	6	89–90	Musical (Britain)
White Cliffs of Dover, The	4	4	57–9	Popular ballad (Britain)
Winter Wonderland	8	5	113	Popular (USA)
Work-a-day Mornin' Blues	3	3	42	Blues (USA)
World Keeps Turning Around, The	8	1	105–6	Children's song (Britain)
Worried Man	1	5	21–2	Traditional (USA)
You'll Never Walk Alone	1	3 and 4	12–13	Musical (USA)

Vocal warm-up exercises and listening extracts

	chapter	lesson	page	activity
Breathing exercise	1	6	17	warm-up
Calypso improvisation	5	2	66	warm-up
Calypso listening	5	2	66	listening
Christmas warm-up	6	2	80	warm-up
Coffee warm-up legato	2	1	25	warm-up
Coffee warm-up staccato	2	1	25	warm-up
Crescendo humming	1	3	9	warm-up
Don't You Rock Me Daddy-O (skiffle song)	7	4	100	listening
Dona Nobis warm-up	2	3	30	warm-up
El Concierto rhythm warm-up	7	1	92	warm-up
Evening warm-up 1	5	1	63	warm-up
Evening warm-up 2	5	1	63	warm-up
Fishing improvisation	7	2	94	listening
Fishing warm-up	7	2	94	warm-up
Geordie's warm-up	4	2	51	warm-up
Gossip warm-up 1	4	1	48	warm-up
Gossip warm-up 2	4	1	48	warm-up
High Notes warm-up	5	4	72	warm-up
Instrumental Backing	8	4	110	listening
Jikel 'Emaweni warm-up	4	2	51	warm-up
Languages warm-up	7	1	92	warm-up
Mistletoe and Wine rhythm patterns	7	3	99	warm-up
Ostinato Pattern 1	1	3	10	warm-up
Ostinato Pattern 2	1	3	10	warm-up
Ostinato Pattern 3	1	3	10	warm-up
Ostinato Pattern 4	1	3	10	warm-up
Oxum rhythm patterns	4	5	60	listening
Rhythm warm-up	3	1	36	warm-up
Scale warm-up	5	5	73	warm-up
Scat improvisation	3	3	41	listening
Songs of the West Patter	2	4	33	warm-up
Syncopation warm-up	7	5	101	warm-up
Syntax Error warm-up	2	2	27	warm-up
Thank You for the Music spoken	6	5	85	warm-up
Thousand Lights warm-up	6	3	82	warm-up
Three parts warm-up	4	3	55	warm-up
Vesper warm-up	6	1	77	warm-up

Glossary

ABA structure

a musical plan that has 3 sections: sections 1 and 3 are the same; section 2 is different

accelerando

getting faster

accent

a note, beat or pulse played or sung with more emphasis than those around it

accompaniment

music that supports the sound of the featured performer(s)

aria

italian word for 'song', in opera

articulation

clear enunciation of words

beat

a repeating pulse

call and response

a song in which two singers or groups sing alternately, the second responding to the call of the first

canon

one voice (or instrument) is imitated, note for note, by a second voice which enters later with the same melody, overlapping the first voice

chord

three or more different notes played together

chord sequence

a succession of chords. The chord sequence can be repeated and often provides the harmonic structure of a song

chorus

see 'refrain'

counter-melody

a melody that weaves in and out of the main melody and is sung at the same time

crescendo

getting louder

cumulative

a song in which a new line is added to each successive verse

decrescendo

getting quieter

diminuendo

gradually getting quieter

diphthong

two vowel sounds pronounced as one syllable

drone

a continuous or repeated pitch or pitches

dynamics

the loudness and quietness of sound

ensemble

any combination of performers

the ensemble

the quality of a group performance, e.g. unanimity of attack, balance, tone

expression marks

symbols used to indicate how music should be performed: here are some common ones
p quietly (from Italian 'piano')
pp very quietly
mp moderately quiet (from Italian 'mezzo piano')
f loudly (from Italian 'forte')
ff very loudly
mf moderately loud (from Italian 'mezzo forte')
crescendo or *cresc.* or ◁ get louder
decrescendo or *decresc.* or ▷ get quieter

Sounds of Singing

rallentando or *rall.* get slower
accelerando or *accel.* get faster

glottal stop

a consonant sound produced by opening or shutting the glottis

glottis

the entrance to the windpipe

gospel song

a religious (Christian) song in a jazz or blues style, originating in the USA

graphic score

a representation of musical sounds using pictures, etc., rather than notation

improvisation

the art of making up and performing music, according to the inventive whim of the moment

intonation

the accurate pitching of musical notes

jazz

a style that grew out of the music of black Americans, then took many different substyles: ragtime, blues, Dixieland, cool jazz, swing bebop, rock, etc. It features solo improvisations over a set harmonic progression

leap

moving from one pitch to another, skipping the pitches in between, e.g. from D to G (see 'step')

legato

smoothly

metre

organisation of strong and weak beats (usually in 2s or 3s)

musical

popular stage show involving singing, drama, speech and dance, in costume

notation

the way in which music can be written down

note

symbols for sound in music (sometimes used as an alternative to 'pitch (1)')

note values

○ = 4   ♩ = 2   ♩ = 1   ♪ = ½   ♪ = ¼

opera

dramatic show with singing, usually no speech, in costume

oratorio

religious (usually Christian) work for solo singers, chorus and orchestra

ostinato

a rhythm or melody pattern that is repeated many times, usually as an accompaniment

pentatonic

music based on a 5-pitch scale, e.g. CDEGA

percussion

instruments that are played by striking with beaters or by shaking

phrase

a musical 'sentence', sometimes marked by ⌒ over the notation

pitch (1)

a single musical sound (sometimes called 'note')

pitch (2)

the highness or lowness of sound

pitched percussion

percussion instruments which produce a specific pitch or pitches, e.g. chime bar

pulse

see 'beat'

rallentando

getting slower

recitative

'sung speech' in an opera or oratorio

refrain

the part of a song that repeats, with the same melody and words (see 'verse')

repetition

music that is the same, or almost the same, as music that was heard earlier

rest

silence between musical sounds

rest values

🎵 = 4   🎵 = 2   𝄽 = 1   𝄾 = 1/2   𝄿 = 1/4

rhythm

the organisation of beat, no beat, long and short sounds, metre, tempo, etc.

round

a vocal perpetual canon, in which the voices sing the same melody but enter in turn

scat singing

jazz singing, improvised freely on syllables such as 'Doo-bi-doo-bi-doo'.

sequence

a phrase repeated but with a different starting pitch

spiritual

a religious song originating in the African American tradition

staccato

short and detached, indicated by a dot immediately above or below a note

staff

set of 5 lines on which music notes are placed to indicate pitch

staggered breathing

a technique used in choral singing. Each singer takes a breath at a different place during an extra-long phrase

stave

see staff

steady beat

regular pulse – the children clap 'in time'

step

moving from one pitch to the next, e.g. from B to C, or from F to F# (see leap)

structure

the overall plan of a piece of music

syncopation

placing a strong emphasis on the weak, or 'off' beat

tempo

the speed of the beat in music (fast, slow)

timbre

special quality (colour) of a sound – a flute has a different timbre from a violin

tuned percussion

see 'pitched percussion'

unaccompanied

see 'accompaniment'

unison

everyone singing or playing the same melody together

verse

the part of a song that repeats with the same melody but different words (see 'refrain')

vocals

singing

528457

Acknowledgements

Diwali Song
Words and music by George Odam © Silver Burdett Ginn

Ebony Trousers
English words by George Odam, words and music by Otto Müller-Blum © Musikverlag Zum Pelikan, Hug & Co.

Everybody's Got a Little Rhythm
Words and music by Peter Combe © Bacalunga Music

Fishing
Traditional/Words by Nick Curtis © Glenda Curtis

Gossip
Words and music by Nick Curtis © Glenda Curtis

Mistletoe and Wine
Words by Leslie Stewart and Jeremy Paul, music by Keith Strachan © 1988 Patch Music Ltd. All rights administered by Peermusic (UK) Ltd, 8-14 Verulam Street, London WC1. Used by permission of Music Sales Ltd. All Rights Reserved. International Copyright Secured.

Notin' Around
Words and music by Shena Power © Georgian Music DTP

River, River
Words and music by Peter Combe © Bacalunga Music

Syncopation
Words and music by George Odam © Georgian Music DTP

Syntax Error
Words and music by Peter Combe © Bacalunga Music

The Termite
Ogden Nash © J.M. Dent & Sons

Thank You for the Music
Words and music by Benny Andersson and Bjorn Ulvaeus © Bocu Music Ltd

Turn, Turn, Turn
Words and music by Pete Seeger © TRO Essex Music Ltd

We're Going to the Country
Words and music by Lionel Bart © 1962 EMI United Partnership Ltd, London WC2H 0EA. Worldwide print rights controlled by Warner Bros Publications Inc/IMP Ltd.

The White Cliffs of Dover
Words by Nat Burton, music by Walter Kent © 1941 Shapiro Bernstein & Co. Inc., USA. Reproduced by permission of B Feldman & Co Ltd, London WC2H 0EA.

Winter Wonderland
Words by Dick Smith, music by Felix Bernard © Francis, Day & Hunter Ltd and Redwood Music Ltd

Work-a-day Mornin' Blues
Words by Rosemary Jacques, music by Sol Berkowitz © Silver Burdett Ginn/CBS Records

The World Keeps Turning Around
Words and music by Susan Stevens © 1980 Reproduced by permission of EMI Music Publishing Ltd, London WC2H 0EA.

You'll Never Walk Alone
Words by Oscar Hammerstein II, music by Richard Rodgers © 1945 by Williamson Music. Copyright renewed. International Copyright Secured. All Rights Reserved.

Every effort has been made to trace all the copyright holders, but if any have been inadvertently overlooked, the publishers will be pleased to make the necessary arrangements at the first opportunity.